Simply Effective Cognitive Behaviour Therapy

A practitioner's guide

Michael J. Scott

Routledge
Taylor & Francis Group

LONDON AND NEW YORK

First published 2009
by Routledge
27 Church Road, Hove, East Sussex BN3 2FA

Simultaneously published in the USA and Canada
by Routledge
270 Madison Avenue, New York, NY 10016

Reprinted 2010

Routledge is an imprint of the Taylor & Francis Group,
an informa business

Typeset in Times by
RefineCatch Limited, Bungay, Suffolk
Printed and bound in Great Britain by
TJ International Ltd, Padstow, Cornwall
Paperback cover design by Aubergine Creative Design

This publication has been produced with paper manufactured to
strict environmental standards and with pulp derived from
sustainable forests.

British Library Cataloguing in Publication Data
A catalogue record for this book is available from the British Library

Library of Congress Cataloging-in-Publication Data
Scott, Michael J., 1948–
    Simply effective cognitive behaviour therapy : a practitioner's guide /
Michael J. Scott.
        p. cm.
    Includes bibliographical references and index.
    1. Cognitive therapy.   2. Behavior therapy.   I. Title.
    RC489.C63S365 2009
    616.89'1425—dc22

                                                        2008043401

ISBN: 978-0-415-46676-9 (hbk)
ISBN: 978-0-415-46677-6 (pbk)

Contents

Chapter 1

Simple CBT – strengths and limitations

Cognitive behaviour therapy (CBT) teaches clients skills to manage their emotional distress. The content of the teaching varies from disorder to disorder. However, the teaching takes place via Socratic questioning, a form of indirect questioning leaving the client to draw their own conclusions. There is no direct challenge to a client's core beliefs or values. Like a teacher the CBT practitioner not only requires technical knowledge of the subject matter, e.g. of the key type of client thinking involved in a particular disorder, but also has to be able to relate and communicate effectively. The spirit of CBT is one of what Beck has termed 'collaborative empiricism' (Beck *et al.* 1979: 79), i.e. rather than the therapist–client relationship being one of 'sage' to 'pupil', agreements are sought as to the testing out of possible ways forward. The skills required of a cognitive behaviour therapist have been summarised in the Cognitive Therapy Rating Scale (Young and Beck 1980). The session by session procedures (protocols) to be followed for the different disorders are outlined in Beck *et al.* (1979) for depression, and in Wells (1997) for panic disorder, social phobia, generalised anxiety disorder and obsessive compulsive disorder. Somewhat strangely, these tried and tested protocols are rarely taught on training courses or implemented by practitioners; this book is an aid to rectifying this omission.

The target audience for this volume are therapists on foundation to intermediate cognitive behaviour therapy courses. Whilst a text is a useful resource in learning a new skill, it is not a substitute for seeing the skill demonstrated then having the opportunity to practise this skill under supervision before independent practice. Importantly this volume contains extensive transcripts of sessions, which can be role played and then 'paused' at a juncture to allow a different student the opportunity to take over as therapist. The results can then be compared with the dialogue that followed in the transcript. Training courses are likely to deliver relatively few competent practitioners unless CBT skills are first modelled, then the student is given feedback in the implementation of the skill before independent practice.

The 'simple CBT' approach advocated is meant to be intensely practical and as such it takes into account that in routine practice clients rarely present with just one disorder. Thus the case studies described in this volume are of clients with more than one disorder and homework assignments are set simultaneously for each disorder.

In 2006 Beck wrote: 'The biggest problems of the present time are in the implementation and dissemination of the empirically validated therapies and the training of therapists to apply them . . . unless some organised effort is made . . . to foster such training and implementation . . . therapies will be available only for a small fraction of those individuals who need them.' His concerns were taken up in the same year in the United Kingdom with the launching of the Improving Access to Psychological Therapies (IAPT) pro- gramme by the Department of Health and in 2007, the Department under the authorship of Anthony D. Roth and Stephen Pilling produced an explana- tory leaflet about CBT for would-be service users. The wider dissemination of CBT in both the United States and the United Kingdom is a key pressing issue. Fortunately at the time of writing (August 2008) the UK Government is spending £306 million, over the next three years, to increase the number of practitioners by 3,600. However, improved access is not just about increasing the number of practitioners, it is also about ensuring the implementation of a CBT approach that is simple, straightforward, effective and in which a variety of modes of service delivery, e.g. individual therapy, self-help, group therapy and computer-assisted therapy, are called upon to ensure maximum efficiency. If CBT is not kept simple then in effect access to effective treatment will continue to be denied.

Where the action is

The key therapeutic target in CBT are cognitions (thoughts/images), and the cognitive theory of emotional disorders (Alford and Beck 1997) suggests that they play a pivotal role in the development and maintenance of emotional disorders. Further the theory suggests that different disorders have a different cognitive content (cognitive content specificity); e.g. in depression the view of the personal world is negative whilst in anxiety it is of being dangerous. The differing cognitive architecture of disorders has led to different treatment protocols.

'Think straight and all will be well': whilst this is a caricature of the cognitive theory of emotional disorders it does convey a central tenet of the theory (Alford and Beck 1997) that 'cognitions', i.e. inferences about one's experiences and about the occurrence and control of future events, are a central pathway to psychological functioning or adaptation. Cognitive behavioural treatments were developed with particular cognitive contents in mind, i.e. they are disorder specific. Thus for example the CBT treatment of post-traumatic stress disorder differs in many ways from that for general- ised anxiety disorder. The cognitive distortions implicated in an emotional disorder may relate to content, e.g. viewing self as worthless, or process, e.g. black and white thinking – success or failure.

Cognitions in context

Cognitions (thoughts and images) influence and are influenced by our behaviour, emotions and physiology. If each of these are viewed as family members then cognitions are just one family member, who like the other family members all affect each other. The 'family' is in turn affected by the outside climate. The interactions are shown in Figure 1.1; for convenience the climate is shown as interacting with the 'family' via cognitions but it could just as easily be via any other family member.

For example, going clockwise around the bottom half of Figure 1.1, if I think (cognition) that writing this paragraph is going to be too difficult I might postpone it by going out to lunch first (behaviour) but I might experience anxiety (emotion) that by so doing I am going to miss a deadline and feel tense (physiology). Feeling tense when I return home might lead me to think (cognition) 'I need a beer to unwind' (completing the circle back to cognition). In turn, having a beer (behaviour) would affect my physiology (horizontal arrow pointing left).

Systems outside the person, here termed the 'climate', such as critical

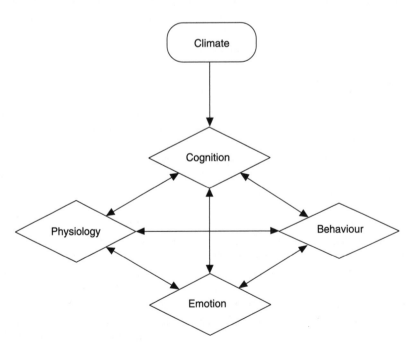

Figure 1.1 Cognitions in context.

significant others and psychosocial stressors (e.g. poor housing, unemployment) also influence the operation of the person and their constituent parts, i.e. cognition, emotion, behaviour and physiology. In the example given above my initial cognition that writing this paragraph would be too difficult may have arisen from a hypercritical 'climate' at home as a child. In some instances it may be more appropriate to address a maladaptive climate–person interaction via relationship therapy than via one of the partner's depressogenic thinking.

Keeping it simple

There is a mnemonic, KISS, which, perhaps to one's surprise, actually stands for 'Keep It Simple Stupid' and is a useful piece of advice to follow if one has to give a talk. It is as if Beck had anticipated 'KISS' thirty years ago and introduced it into the baffling world of psychotherapy. For the first time there were signposts about what needed doing in a therapy session, e.g. agreeing an agenda, setting homework, reviewing homework. Further CBT was brief compared to existing psychotherapies and was complete with session by session descriptions of what needed doing. The hallmark of CBT was a simplicity which made it very attractive and facilitated dissemination. Whilst thirty years on CBT has achieved a pre-eminence amongst the psychotherapies, students or practitioners rarely refer to its simplicity and oftentimes appear overawed by a perceived complexity. Hopefully this volume will empower students and established practitioners alike by elaborating what can be achieved quite simply and what cannot.

CBT works

The success of cognitive behaviour therapy has been reflected in the National Institute for Health and Clinical Excellence recommendations (e.g. NICE 2004) of CBT as the treatment of choice for a wide range of disorders. In some of the studies of CBT its effects have been compared with how people fared on a waiting list for treatment. The average client who underwent CBT outperformed most clients on the waiting list. In Table 1.1 the proportions outperformed for each disorder are summarised.

Inspection of Table 1.1 shows that CBT is highly effective for the most common mental disorders. (For panic disorder and post-traumatic stress disorder different researchers have employed different outcome measures, resulting in slightly different proportions depending on the particular outcome measure under consideration.) The studies of obsessive compulsive disorder (OCD) and bulimia reviewed by Butler *et al.* (2006) did not involve comparisons of CBT to a waiting list, but focused on reduction of symptoms from pre to post treatment. Whilst they did show that most clients with these conditions improved, OCD (58–97%) and bulimia (89–91%), with such a

Table 1.1 Proportion of patients on waiting list
outperformed by the average client completing CBT, by
disorder (Adapted from Butler *et al.* 2006)

Depression	79%
Generalised anxiety disorder	79%
Panic disorder with agoraphobia	59–69%
Panic disorder with or without agoraphobia	74–90%
Social phobia	82%
Post-traumatic stress disorder	83–96%

research design it can be objected that there would have been some naturally occurring improvement anyway and there is less certainty that the effect was due to CBT. Notwithstanding the weaker methodology of the bulimia and OCD studies, CBT appears to have promise for these conditions.

The Butler *et al.* (2006) review of studies also found significant evidence for the long-term effectiveness of CBT for depression, generalised anxiety disorder (GAD), panic disorder, social phobia and OCD. In the case of depression and panic the relapse rate after CBT is half that with pharmaco-therapy. In addition, CBT appears to show greater long-term effects in the treatment of GAD as compared to applied relaxation.

Lost in translation?

The good news is that when the evidence-based protocols that the research studies in Table 1.1 are based on have been applied in ordinary clinical set-tings, they have been of comparable effectiveness. For example, Wade *et al.* (1998) applied Barlow and Craske's (1994) efficacious treatment for panic disorder to a service clinic setting. They trained the already existing therapists there to administer a standard protocol and improvements were comparable to changes observed with the same treatment programme in efficacy studies. However, the authors reported that the dropout rate was higher than that in efficacy studies, although still considerably lower than the dropout rate usu-ally observed on community mental health centre samples. Chambless and Ollendick (2001) reviewed five studies of the effectiveness of CBT for depres-sion in routine clinical practice and found positive results. Interestingly two of the studies were of a standardised group cognitive behaviour therapy for depression in low-income outpatients and 62–80% (depending on ethnicity) no longer met diagnostic criteria for depression after treatment. However, the dropout rate was higher with this disadvantaged population (40–60%) than in efficacy studies (e.g. 32%, Elkin *et al.* 1989). At an inner city health centre in Toxteth, Liverpool, Ross and Scott (1985) compared the effectiveness of individual and group cognitive therapy for depression and found both were equally effective and superior to a waiting list control condition. In an expanded study Scott and Stradling (1990) found that group cognitive therapy for depression produced clinically significant reliable change in community-based settings. Most research is, however, conducted in research centres and is focused on establishing the efficacy of a CBT treatment, and comparatively little research has been conducted on the effectiveness of CBT in practice. Despite the need for more effectiveness studies, funding is difficult to obtain. However, the results so far are encouraging.

There is a tendency to dismiss the relevance of research studies to routine clinical practice on the grounds that the clients seen in the latter context are very different. However, the crucial question is whether a particular client is sufficiently like a set of clients who have benefited from an empirically supported treatment, that the latter should be the treatment of choice. In a research study clients are assessed using a structured interview (most usually the SCID, First *et al.* 1997), in which clients are asked about each symptom that comprises a diagnostic set and there are guidelines as to what type of information would be required for a symptom to be considered present. The levels of agreement between different assessors in research studies is about 90%, i.e. there is very strong agreement about which disorders are present. However, in routine clinical practice structured interviews are rarely used and levels of agreement are 32–54% (Beck *et al.* 1962). Thus because of the non-use of a structured interview in routine practice it is not possible to reliably know whether a client is a match for a particular protocol. Asserting that an evidence-based intervention is not appropriate for a client, without a diagnostic assessment, is an unfounded assumption.

The usual restrictions in efficacy outcome studies are that the client should not be actively suicidal, psychotic or alcohol/drug dependent. Apart from these considerations clients are usually entered into the study with additional diagnoses (co-morbidity), provided the disorder under study is the principal reason they are seeking help. Thus the studies on which Table 1.1 is based cover a broad spectrum of the clients attending in routine clinical practice. The research studies can be translated to routine practice but with some caution.

Painting by numbers?

The use of manuals/protocols has been likened to 'painting by numbers' by Silverman (1996) and Smith (1995) has referred to their use as representing 'a cookbook mentality'. These disparaging comments have found a resonance for those who perceive a manualised approach threatening their independence of practice and creativity. In this atmosphere it is not surprising that the protocols are rarely taught on training courses or used to guide routine clinical practice. But there is no evidence that those who have used the manuals have found themselves constricted. This is not at all surprising when it is borne in mind that for a therapist to have been acceptable for an efficacy study they need to have demonstrated competence on the Cognitive Therapy Rating Scale (CTRS). Highest scores on the CTRS are given for items that include: feedback 'therapist was especially adept at eliciting and responding to verbal and non-verbal feedback throughout the session'; interpersonal effectiveness 'therapist displayed optimal levels of warmth, concern, confidence, genuineness and professionalism'; collaboration 'function as a team'; guided discovery 'especially adept at using guided discovery'; application of cognitive behavioural techniques 'therapist very skilfully and resourcefully employed cognitive-behavioural techniques'; and additional considerations 'therapist was very skilful at handling special problems using the cognitive therapy framework'. Therapists would have failed on the CTRS if indeed they were operating in a cookbook-like way or without creativity and warmth. There can be no better role model for practitioners than the therapists who have partaken in the research studies.

Special considerations

Whilst probably most clients presenting at a primary care level would benefit from one or more of the CBT protocols presented in this book there are a minority for whom they would be inappropriate. The protocols in this volume were not developed for clients with psychosis, substance dependence or personality disorder. This group of clients can be a risk to themselves and more rarely to others. It is important therefore for therapists to routinely gauge the level of risk of all clients and direct those at risk to the appropriate service.

Unfortunately there is no universally accepted manner of determining risk and the following suggestions are by no means the only way of conducting a risk assessment; they are included here for the sake of completion. Miller and Giordano (2007) have developed a risk-assessment tool using the acronym SAD PERSONS, shown in Table 1.2.

One point is assigned to each of the ten items identified as risk factors for suicide in Table 1.2. A score of one or two points indicates low risk, three to

Table 1.2 Risk-assessment tool (Miller and Giordano 2007)

- **S**ex (male)
- **A**ge less than 19 or greater than 45 years
- **D**epression (patient admits to depression or decreased concentration, sleep, appetite and/or libido)
- **P**revious suicide attempt or psychiatric care
- **E**xcessive alcohol or drug use
- **R**ational thinking loss: psychosis, organic brain syndrome
- **S**eparated, divorced or widowed
- **O**rganised plan or serious attempt
- **N**o social support
- **S**ickness, chronic disease

five points indicates moderate risk, and seven to ten signals high risk. The results of the SAD PERSONS should be discussed in supervision and certainly those at high risk should be referred on and consideration should be given to whether those at moderate risk should be referred on. The virtue of the SAD PERSONS is that it keeps a therapist mindful of the important considerations with regard to suicide risk.

The sense of hopelessness is a better predictor of suicidal behaviour than severity of depression and is considered a pre-eminent risk factor for suicide and non-fatal self-harm (see McMillan *et al.* 2007). It is also a source of concern if a person cannot elaborate a reason for living, e.g. grandchildren. Other key predictors of eventual suicide for suicide attempters include their regret over the failure of the suicide attempt and increasing intensity of their suicidal ideation with each successive attempt.

Risk assessment may be documented using the Galatean Risk Screening Tool (GRiST), which is available free on the web at www.galassify.org/grist. This assessment begins with biographic details, followed by a two-page screening questionnaire that covers suicide, self-harm, harm to others or damage to property, self-neglect and vulnerability of service user. If the therapist answers yes to a screening question then they are directed to more detailed questioning for the particular concern. The GRiST is designed for non-specialist frontline staff. At the time of writing (August 2008), there is not as yet published guidance on how the various items should be weighted, i.e. on risk quantification. However, the GRiST does help to standardise risk assessment and highlights the important domains, and its authors are intending to produce a risk quantification.

The good news is that cognitive therapy appears to reduce repeat suicide attempts by 50%. In a study by Brown *et al.* (2005), patients who had made a suicide attempt were given either a ten-session cognitive therapy programme or enhanced usual care and both groups were followed up for 18 months. Only 24.1% in the cognitive therapy group compared to 41.6% in the usual care group made at least one subsequent suicide attempt. The cognitive therapy focused on countering feelings of hopelessness and on the events, thoughts and behaviours that led to their previous suicide attempts and the distillation of more adaptive responses. If the client was successful at generating a new coping strategy the therapy ended; if unsuccessful, additional sessions were added. However, such a cognitive therapy programme, though extremely important, would not fall under the umbrella of simple CBT and is not detailed in this volume.

Functional impairment

There is a consensus that the protocols for depression and anxiety disorders are appropriate for clients with mild to moderate mental health problems. Further the first level of psychological services in the UK generally has as its target clients with mild to moderate mental health problems. However, there are no universally agreed criteria for 'mild to moderate mental health problems', and the blurred boundary means that many first line teams and charities often find themselves under pressure to cater for 'serious cases' at a potential considerable cost to their core service. There is a need for an operational definition of the severity labels. In some instances the term 'severe mental illness' is used to denote a condition, e.g. schizophrenia or bipolar disorder, in which a psychosis is likely to occur. Community Mental Health Teams often define themselves as devoted to clients with a psychosis and Primary Care Services as concerned with patients with mild to moderate mental health problems; this can leave patients who have been suicidal or self-harming in the absence of psychosis falling between two stools. There is a need for highly skilled CBT practitioners devoted to those who self-harm and whose functioning is severely affected by personality disorder; unfortunately the location of services for such complex cases has become a funding football.

One way of delineating who is appropriate for which service is to use the Global Assessment of Functioning (GAF) Scale in DSM-IV-TR (American Psychiatric Association 2000: 34). The GAF is a measure of a client's overall functioning. To arrive at a score the therapist considers the client's psychological, social and occupational functioning on a hypothetical continuum of mental health–illness. The therapist must *not* take into account impairment in functioning due to physical or environmental limitations. The scale ranges from 1 to 100, with scores in the band 91–100 representing superior functioning in a wide range of activities and scores in the band 1–10 representing persistent danger of severely hurting self or others. An extract from the GAF is shown in Table 1.3.

Within each band consideration is given to both symptoms and impairment in functioning, and the GAF rating given always reflects the worse of the two. Thus the protocols in this book would seem most appropriate for clients with GAF scores greater than 50. The GAF can be used as a comprehensive measure of global mental health in routine clinical work for

Table 1.3 Extract from GAF (DSM-IV-TR, American Psychiatric Association 2000: 34)

70–61	Some mild symptoms (e.g. depressed mood and mild insomnia or some difficulty in social, occupational, or school functioning but generally functioning pretty well, has some meaningful interpersonal relationships
60–51	Moderate symptoms (e.g. flat affect and circumstantial speech, occasional panic attacks) or moderate difficulty in social, occupational or school functioning (e.g. few friends, conflict with peers or co-workers)
50–41	Serious symptoms (e.g. suicidal ideation, severe obsessional rituals, frequent shoplifting) or any serious impairment in social, occupational or school functioning (e.g. no friends, unable to keep a job)

assessment and for outcome management (see Tungstrom *et al.* 2005). Online free training in the use of the GAF is provided at the website Washington Institute Mental Illness Research and Training CGAS GAF where a full copy of the GAF can be downloaded (www.wimirt.washington.edu).

The evidence that severity of presenting problem affects outcome was reviewed by an expert panel in the Department of Health document 'Treatment Choice in Psychological Therapies and Counselling' (2001) and they concluded that in fact the results were equivocal. For depression a combination of greater severity, chronicity and earlier first onset tends to predict higher residual symptoms at the end of therapy (Agosti and Ocepek-Welikson 1997) which in turn increases the risk of relapse (Hamilton and Dobson 2002).

The effects of coexisting personality disorders

Although there is a consensus in the Department of Health (2001) document that the coexistence of a personality disorder and depression leads to a poorer outcome, the evidence supporting this belief is not strong (see Roth and Fonagy 2005: 130 for a review). Weertman *et al.* (2005) examined whether having a personality disorder affected the success of CBT treatment for anxiety clients (the 398 patients in their study met diagnostic criteria for variously: agoraphobia, panic disorder with agoraphobia, panic disorder without agoraphobia, specific phobia, generalised anxiety disorder, obsessive compulsive disorder, post-traumatic stress disorder, social phobia and anxiety disorder not otherwise specified) and found that those with personality disorders (37%) reported higher symptom levels at outcome. However, these effects were not as strong as might be expected on the basis of the prevailing clinical wisdom. Dropout rates were not influenced by whether the client had a personality disorder. Weertman *et al.* (2005) concluded that treatment of anxiety disorders in clients with one or more personality disorders is appropriate. However, 1.5% of Weertman's subjects had a borderline personality disorder; these clients are particularly challenging in that they have difficulties in maintaining relationships, often making therapy fraught, and are often impulsive and sometimes self-destructive. These complex cases are best dealt with using treatments such as dialectical behaviour therapy (Linehan 1993) and are beyond the scope of simple CBT.

Chapter 2

Getting started – diagnosis and beyond

It was not until the pioneering work of Aaron T. Beck, the founder of cognitive therapy, that psychological treatments became diagnosis specific. In order to evaluate the efficacy of a treatment, manuals were developed for each disorder. The key features of manuals are summarised in Table 2.1.

Thus a manualised approach provides an easy focus for training and supervision. It is also a reference point in determining whether appropriate therapy has been conducted.

Talking the same language

One of Beck's earliest publications focused on making psychiatric diagnoses more reliable (Beck *et al.* 1962). Beck and his colleagues found that the level of agreement about whether a person had a particular disorder varied between 32% and 54%. This made researching the effectiveness of treatments near impossible because a particular client might be described by one person as suffering from depression but another assessor would give a quite different label. To help ensure good levels of agreement, Beck drew attention to the importance of minimising (a) information variance – the range of information considered important in making a particular diagnosis and (b) criteria variance – the information needed to establish the presence or absence of a particular symptom. This led to the publication of agreed criteria for each disorder, currently embodied in DSM-IV-TR (American Psychiatric Association 2000) and published guidance on the thresholds needed to determine whether a particular symptom can be regarded as present (SCID, First *et al.*

Table 2.1 Manual characteristics

1. The theoretical background for a treatment
2. The rationale for clients
3. The procedures to be used including session by session guidelines
4. Specific prompts and suggestions to be used to implement the procedures and address patient issues that hinder implementation of the protocol

1997). Using structured interviews such as the SCID, levels of agreement rise to 90% for most disorders, ensuring almost all are singing from the same hymn sheet. Clients in most of the cognitive therapy trials have usually been assessed using the SCID or an alternative structured interview, the ADIS (Brown *et al.* 2004). Beck's seminal work on diagnostic accuracy paved the way for the development of different protocols or procedures for different disorders.

DSM-IV-TR (American Psychiatric Association 2000: xxxii) states that proper use of the diagnostic criteria involves directly accessing information in the criteria set. This is achieved in this volume by first screening clients for common mental health disorders using either an interview 'The 7 Minute Mental Health Screen' (Appendix C) or, to save time even further, the self-report version, 'The First Step Questionnaire' (Appendix H), which takes clients just 2–3 minutes to complete. These measures highlight candidate disorders. Then detailed enquiry is made of the 'candidates' using the relevant sections of the 'Cognitive Behaviour Therapy Pocketbook' in Appendix D. The Pocketbook is for use in the same way as the SCID or ADIS in that it is important that the assessor does not use the suggested questions simply as a checklist, accepting a client's 'yes' or 'no' response without clarification. It is of key importance to determine, on the basis of what the client has said (concrete examples are needed) and any other information available, e.g. from partner or records, that the client is significantly functionally impaired with regard to that symptom. For example, a depressed client may well report being forgetful or having memory lapses, but in order to determine whether impaired concentration is endorsed as present, it would be important to know whether the concentration difficulties are having an effect on their work performance or enjoyment of TV/DVDs/reading; only if they were would the symptom be regarded as present at a clinically significant level.

Vectors for cognitive-behavioural treatment

A vector is a mathematical term indicating a quantity with a magnitude and a direction. Diagnosis may be likened to a vector in that diagnosis-specific CBT has been shown to be effective, i.e. it has a magnitude/makes a difference and the protocols for the different disorders have a direction, e.g. session by session guidance. However, diagnosis is rather like a compass: it indicates the general direction in which to go but does not indicate a particular path. The specific path is indicated by another vector, case formulation, which is an example of a 'case', of a disorder. Thus a person might be suffering from depression, but the way in which that individual expresses their depression will be different to another's. For example, for one depressed client inappropriate guilt may be an important issue whilst for another it is not, yet they are both depressed.

The case formulation is the therapist's working hypothesis of how the client came to be suffering from their current problems and to present at this particular point in time. Both vectors, diagnosis and case formulation, are required for effective treatment; together they give quite a different direction to either alone.

Weerasekera (1996) has detailed the components of case formulation and they are expressed in tabular form and adapted in Table 2.2.

Thus Table 2.2 might be used to chart the development and maintenance of, say, a client's post-traumatic stress disorder (PTSD) following a road traffic accident (RTA). With regard to predisposing factors, whilst the individual (column 2 in Table 2.2) might not have had a previous mental health problem they might be judged slightly more vulnerable than most to the effects of a trauma because at an environmental level there is a family history of psychological illness. A recent RTA (operating at an individual level) might be judged as precipitating the PTSD; however, if the client also lost their partner in the RTA, this would likely also be regarded as a precipitating factor but operating at an environmental level. Utilising a cognitive behavioural model of PTSD (see, for example, Scott and Stradling 2006), the perpetuating factor would likely be the client's avoidance of driving, which prevents disconfirmation of their belief that driving is tantamount to manoeuvring in a war zone. A further perpetuating factor operating at an environmental level might be a family taboo on discussing the accident. Protective factors operating at an environmental level might be a supportive family or at an individual level the client may have hitherto displayed high levels of learned resourcefulness/resilience in dealing with major negative life events. The case formulation would inform treatment by the therapist seeking to nullify the perpetuating factors and capitalise on the protective factors.

A case formulation is necessary for each identified disorder and the therapist would need to integrate the formulations to chart a direction. Thus for example the client depicted in Table 2.2 might be suffering not only from PTSD but also from depression. The therapist might draw on a CBT model

Table 2.2 Components of case formulation

	Individual	Environmental
Predisposing factors, e.g. family history of psychological illness		
Precipitating factors, e.g. recent road traffic accident		
Perpetuating factors, e.g. avoidance of reminders of road traffic accident		
Protective factors, e.g. supportive family		

of depression developed by Champion and Power (1995), which posits that depression can develop from the loss of an overvalued role, to hypothesise that this client's depression arises from, say, his inability ever to do his much valued manual job following the RTA. Thus at an individual level the perpetuating factor would be the overvalued role but matters might be compounded at an environmental level if there is no non-manual job for the client to move to. Effective treatment would therefore be a product of an interweave of the PTSD and depression case formulations.

Keeping to the musical score

The protocols that have been found to be so effective in controlled trials are like musical scores written by composers. Therapists may be considered members of the orchestra, all needing to follow the same score for the same piece of music/diagnosis. However, whilst it is necessary to follow a score for an audience to know which piece of music is being played some musicians/ therapists will be more skilful than others. Thus the CBT practitioner is as much a craftsman as technician, both are essential.

The dangers of attempting CBT without diagnoses (generic CBT) are summarised in Table 2.3.

Using unstructured interviews, Zimmerman et al. (2008) found that three-quarters of clients were given just one diagnosis. However, using a structured interview (SCID, First et al. 1997), 50–75% of clients receiving a diagnosis of PTSD, GAD, OCD, depression, social phobia and panic disorder (with or without agoraphobia) met criteria for at least one additional diagnosis. Consequently a generic CBT approach is likely to have too narrow a focus. In an earlier study Zimmerman and Mattia (2000) reported that clients want treatment to address the symptoms of their co-morbid disorders. Thus from the client's perspective detecting co-morbid disorders is important.

Without diagnosis a therapist will rely entirely on a case formulation, i.e. make a wholly individual model of the development and maintenance of the client's difficulties. However, following a review of the extent to which different assessors agree with regard to a case formulation, i.e. the low reliability of case formulation, Kuyken et al. (2005) suggested that for straightforward clinical presentations and for therapists early in training better outcomes are

Table 2.3 Dangers of conducting CBT without structured diagnosis

1. Stopping at the first problem/disorder identified
2. Failure to appreciate that a particular CBT strategy was developed with a particular disorder in mind
3. Failure to see client's problems as an example of the cognitive model of a particular disorder, resulting in an overly individualistic approach that is not evidence based

achieved by staying close to protocols and manualised approaches. This is not to say that case formulation does not have a role to play in tailoring a treatment to the individual but that there has to be at least as much emphasis on what the individual is an example of a 'case' of, as on the formulation. Diagnosis outlines treatment whilst formulation refines the details; both are necessary.

Psychometric tests – strengths and pitfalls

Psychometric tests are very good as a measure of the severity of a disorder and for assessing whether a client has improved or deteriorated. For example, in outcome studies of depression the typical mean Beck Depression Inventory (BDI) score of clients entering the studies is about 28 (Scott and Stradling 1990) with a standard deviation of 7 and patients were judged to have fully recovered if their end of treatment score was equal to or less than 9 (i.e. their score had become more like what the average member of the general public might score). For each psychometric test it is possible to calculate how big a change in score has to be in order to be regarded as a clinically significant reliable change using a formula derived by Jacobson and Truax (1991), i.e. a change that is unlikely to have occurred by chance or simply with the passage of time. In order to calculate this figure it is necessary to know both the standard deviation in a clinical sample of the population under study and the test–retest reliability of the instrument (i.e. to what extent people would score the same on the test a short time later). For the actual formula and a worked example see Rosqvist (2005), but there is a free reliable change criterion calculator on the web (www.psyctc.org); using the calculator and entering a standard deviation on the BDI of 7 and a test–retest reliability for the BDI of 0.8 (derived from studies on the BDI where the test–retest interval is short), the calculator informs one that the BDI score has to change by at least 8.7 to be regarded as clinically significant and reliable. But it is necessary of course to know that the client you are focusing on is actually from the same population that was used in the study, i.e. with reference to the BDI that the client initially met diagnostic criteria for depression.

However, psychometric tests are not a substitute for diagnosis. The reason for this is that they tend to generate many false positives, i.e. to suggest that more people have a disorder than actually have it. Technically self-report measures tend to have low specificity. Consequently using a psychometric test for diagnostic purposes can easily mean that the wrong disorder is targeted. For example, Engelhard et al. (2007) asked individuals with post-traumatic stress disorder, other anxiety disorders and healthy controls to complete the PTSD symptom scale (PDS, Foa et al. 1997). The good news was that 86% of individuals with PTSD endorsed sufficient symptoms to meet the PTSD diagnosis. The bad news was that 43% of individuals with other anxiety disorders also endorsed sufficient symptoms to meet the PTSD diagnosis. Thus if a practitioner was relying on the questionnaire almost half the anxiety disorder clients would have been treated inappropriately.

Psychometric tests that tap the cognitions and behaviours that serve to maintain a disorder have a clear clinical utility. For example, a useful measure with regard to generalised anxiety disorder is the Anxious Thoughts Inventory (Wells 1997) which can be used to indicate whether a client's concerns are more social, e.g. 'I worry about my abilities not living up to other people's expectations', or more to do with worry about worry (meta-worry), e.g. 'I worry that I cannot control my thoughts as well as I would like to'. Depending on the client's responses there would be a different emphasis in therapy. Further it would be important to re-administer the measure during therapy to see whether change was occurring in the important cognitive domains.

Making a diagnosis

Probably most therapist referrals will come via a medic, either a GP or a psychiatrist. Symptoms of anxiety and depression can sometimes be due to the direct physiological effects of a general medical condition and a therapist will usually assume that such a possibility has been excluded when a referral has been made. However, if symptoms persist despite an evidence-based CBT treatment, it is not unreasonable for the therapist to suggest to the source of the referral that consideration might be given to an underlying medical condition, e.g. a possible thyroid problem producing the panic-like symptoms. If a client is self-referred the therapist has to be particularly mindful of such possible physical explanations.

The context for diagnosis

The most reliable assessments begin with an open-ended interview followed by a structured interview and psychometric test (see Rogers 2001). It is very rare for the referrer to have conducted all three and in these circumstances the diagnosis made by the source of referral has to be treated with some caution. An open-ended interview allows the client the space to tell their story of what has led them to come to see you now. In such an interview the client will usually detail various psychosocial, e.g. family, problems and environmental, e.g. occupational, problems. These problems provide a context for diagnosis. The DSM-IV-TR has a multi-axial classification system: axis one is reserved for the diagnosis, e.g. obsessive compulsive disorder, and axis four documents psychosocial and environmental problems. A psychosocial/environmental problem checklist is shown in Table 2.4. The checklist allows the therapist to note and follow contextual issues that are important to consider in the ongoing treatment of the client.

Table 2.4 Psychosocial/environmental problem checklist

Family problems   *Specify:*
Other social or interpersonal problems   *Specify:*
Educational problems   *Specify:*
Occupational problems   *Specify:*
Housing problems   *Specify:*
Economic problems   *Specify:*
Problems with access to health care services   *Specify:*
Problems related to interaction with the legal system/crime   *Specify:*
Other psychosocial problems   *Specify:*

In the open-ended interview the client will likely flag up particular symp-toms such as fear, worry, repetitive, intrusive, inappropriate thoughts or actions, sadness, loss of interest, excessive alcohol use. The DSM-IV Primary Care Version (American Psychiatric Association 1995) contains useful algo-rithms for the diagnosis of common mental health problems. Each algorithm begins with a consideration of whether the symptoms observed might not be due to the direct physiological effects of an underlying medical condition. A variety of general medical conditions may directly cause mood symptoms, e.g. Parkinson's disease, stroke, vitamin B12 deficiency, hyper- and hypothy-roidismn, hepatitis, HIV and carcinoma of the pancreas. Whilst it is outside the expertise of a therapist to decide whether a client has any such general medical condition, the therapist needs to be aware of the possibility and consult referrers accordingly. However, because substance abuse is so com-mon, special mention needs to be made of the way in which the withdrawal symptoms from substance abuse, e.g. alcohol, can mimic anxiety symptoms. As a rough rule of thumb recovery from withdrawal symptoms can be expected in about 4 weeks, so that symptoms persisting beyond that point are likely to have a psychological origin.

Substance abuse is often not reported by clients unless directly asked about and it is therefore important to embed a screening test in the assessment, such as CAGE (Ewing 1984) in Table 2.5.

Each yes response to a CAGE question is scored as 1. A total score of 0–4 results from summing positive answers. A score of 2 or higher is considered clinically significant and should raise the therapist's suspicion that the client

Table 2.5 The CAGE questionnaire

C Have you ever felt you should Cut down on your drinking?
A Have people Annoyed you by criticising your drinking?
G Have you ever felt bad or Guilty about your drinking?
E Have you ever had a drink first thing in the morning to steady your nerves or get rid of a hangover (Eye opener)?

has an alcohol-related problem or diagnosis. For males >21 units and for females >14 units a week is regarded as hazardous (half pint beer, glass of wine, glass of sherry, single measure of spirits is 1 unit). When clients are drinking above accepted limits, they should be asked 'what part do you think your drinking is playing in your difficulties?' If substance abuse is a significant factor referral to a specialist agency/unit should be considered. (If a client has a physical disorder but it is not the direct physiological cause of the psychological disorder, the disorder is specified on axis three of DSM-IV.)

Navigating through diagnostic possibilities

The DSM-IV Primary Care Version (American Psychiatric Association 1995) has a series of algorithms to help a therapist clarify the range of diagnostic possibilities and select candidate disorders worthy of further examination. The first step in all the algorithms in DSM-IV is a clarification of whether the symptoms might be due to the direct physiological effect of a general medical condition. As mentioned earlier in this chapter, the therapist can at least in the first instance assume, given that the referral is most likely from a medic, that a largely organic cause of the client's difficulties has already been excluded. Thus the therapist can usually begin at step 2 of the algorithms. As an aid to diagnosis of the anxiety disorders, an adapted version of the DSM-IV algorithm is shown in Table 2.6.

Table 2.6 highlights cardinal features of the differing anxiety disorders. With regard to a diagnosis of depression DSM-IV-TR (American Psychiatric Association 2000) stipulates that a necessary condition is that the person is either depressed and down most of the day on most days and/or has lost interest or pleasure in things that they usually enjoyed.

As mentioned earlier in this chapter, screening questions for each of ten common mental disorders are contained in 'The 7 Minute Mental Screen/ Audit', shown in Appendix C, and in the questionnaire version 'The First Step Questionnaire', Appendix H. The screen takes just 7 minutes and helps ensure that no disorders are missed. The screening questions for depression have been found to correctly identify 79% of those who are depressed and correctly identify 94% of those who are not depressed; importantly, including the question 'Is this something with which you would like help?' greatly reduced the number of false positives (Arroll et al. 2005). This question has therefore been added to the screening for the other disorders. The screening questions for post-traumatic stress disorder (Prins et al. 2004) and substance abuse (Ewing 1984) have also been subjected to empirical investigation and found to be reliable. Further the screening questions for generalised anxiety disorder (GAD) symptoms cover the same content area as the two-item GAD scale that has been demonstrated to have high sensitivity and specificity for detecting GAD (Kroenke et al. 2007). However, at this time the screening questions for other disorders have only a face validity. The self-report version

Table 2.6 Anxiety algorithm

Step 2	If the presenting symptom is recurrent panic attacks consider panic disorder with agoraphobia or panic disorder without agoraphobia or panic attacks occurring within the context of other anxiety disorders (e.g. social phobia, post-traumatic stress disorder, specific phobia, obsessive compulsive disorder)
Step 3	If the presenting symptom is fear, avoidance, or anxious anticipation about one or more specific situations, consider social phobia (avoidance of social situations in which the person may be exposed to scrutiny) or specific phobia (avoidance of a specific object or situation) or panic disorder with agoraphobia (avoidance of situations in which escape may be difficult in the event of a panic attack) or agoraphobia without history of panic disorder (avoidance of a situation in which escape may be difficult in the event of developing panic-like symptoms)
Step 4	If the presenting symptoms include fear of separation, consider separation anxiety disorder (anxiety concerning separation from major attachment figure)
Step 5	If the presenting worry or anxiety is related to recurrent and persistent thoughts (obsessions) and/or ritualistic behaviours or recurrent mental acts (compulsions), consider obsessive compulsive disorder
Step 6	If the presenting symptoms are related to re-experiencing highly traumatic events, consider post-traumatic stress disorder (if symptoms persist at least 4 weeks) or acute stress disorder (if symptoms persist for less than 4 weeks)
Step 7	If pervasive symptoms of anxiety and worry are associated with a variety of events or situations and have persisted for at least 6 months, consider generalised anxiety disorder.

of the screen, 'The First Step Questionnaire', similarly awaits validation; its strength is that it takes the client 2–3 minutes to complete and it takes the therapist only a minute to interpret using the guidance given for the correspondingly numbered items in the 7 Minute Health Screen. If a screen/ questionnaire response for a disorder is positive then more detailed enquiry can be made for that disorder using the questions in Appendix D, the Pocketbook. It is not necessary to examine further for each positive disorder on the screen at the same appointment; the therapist can return to the results of the screen at the next session and then make detailed enquiry of outstanding highlighted disorders.

Additional diagnoses

In a study of 2,300 psychiatric outpatients (Zimmerman *et al.* 2008) the mean number of axis one diagnoses per patient was 1.9, indicating that co-morbidity is commonplace. The term principal diagnosis denotes the disorder that the client indicates as the main reason for seeking treatment; all other diagnoses are considered additional diagnoses. The pattern of co-morbidity varies according to the principal diagnosis. Co-morbidity has generally been found to be associated with a poorer outcome. For example, for obsessive compulsive disorder there are mixed findings on whether severity affects outcome (see Roth and Fonagy 2005: 203 for a review). To the extent that there may be a relationship it is thought that the more severe the disorder, the more likely the client is to have an additional disorder and poorer functioning; the latter two predict a poorer outcome.

As a general rule of thumb the disorders from which the client suffers should be treated simultaneously. However, there are notable exceptions to this rule. If a client is substance dependent, traditionally this has been treated first. Further, if a client is suicidal or engaged in self-harm addressing these concerns should be given priority, albeit that they are beyond simple CBT.

Multi-axial description and case formulation

Diagnosis does not involve a simple labelling of a client. DSM-IV seeks to provide a 3-D view of the client using a multi-axial classification system. On axis one are the mental health disorders, including all those covered in this book. Axis two in DSM-IV is used to indicate the presence of a personality disorder and mental retardation. A potted summary of the ten personality disorders in DSM-IV-TR is shown in Appendix A. They are grouped in three clusters. Cluster A is often referred to as the 'odd' personality disorders, cluster B as the 'dramatic' personality disorders, cluster C as the 'anxious' personality disorders. Appendix A also contains examples of the differing cognitive contents of the personality disorders.

In a study by Weertman et al. (2005) of sufferers from axis one anxiety disorders, 37% had an axis two personality disorder (PD), but although the presence of a PD did affect outcome the effect was small. The cluster C 'anxious' personality disorders were much more common than clusters A and B. In a study of depressed outpatients (Kuyken et al. 2001) undergoing cognitive therapy those with personality disorders did just as well as those without personality disorders. However, the personality disordered patients were more severely depressed at intake and had more residual symptoms at the end of therapy. Nevertheless all therapists need to be alert to the possibility that clients with 'dramatic' and 'odd' personality disorders may present, and the full criteria for personality disorders are available at www.mentalhealth.com.

Axis three of DSM-IV is devoted to a specification of general medical conditions. Axis four in DSM-IV details the psychosocial problems such as housing, relationship problems or finances that provide a context for the disorder. Thus axis four serves to individualise a person's disorder. Axis five documents a client's overall level of functioning using the Global Assessment of Functioning (GAF) Scale discussed in the previous chapter.

The intent of the multi-axial system is to give a rounded description of the individual's difficulties where the focus is not only on what an individual has in common with others but also on what ways they are different to others.

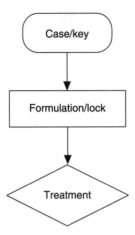

Figure 2.1 Case formulation.

This dual focus leads to a description of a 'case' of a disorder. However, use of the multi-axial system does not directly indicate how the individual has come to be suffering from the disorder and importantly how it is maintained; for this a formulation is needed.

The cognitive theory of emotional disorders (Alford and Beck 1997) states that underlying each disorder there is a specific cognitive behavioural mechanism involved in the development and maintenance of symptoms. A 'formulation' involves integrating the relevant mechanism into the description of the individual's difficulties in order to form a working model of the client's difficulties. It ought always to be possible to test out the accuracy of a model; thus a client with panic disorder might be asked not to put danger labels on every uncomfortable bodily sensation. If they did this but with no reduction in the frequency or intensity of panic attacks this would call the applicability of the model into question and consideration might be given to a medical explanation of their difficulties.

The 'case' and 'formulation' go together like a key and lock: turning the key unlocks the door to specific cognitive behavioural interventions (Fig. 2.1).

However, there are as many 'doors' as disorders present, and for each there will be a different key and lock. Thus case formulation can be used to describe co-morbid disorders, i.e. additional disorders. The doors are rather like taking X-rays of various parts of an injured body, determining what needs to be done where.

Chapter 3

The first interview

Clients usually arrive at the first therapy session demoralised by their lack of success at mastering their difficulties but with a hope that therapy may make a difference. The therapist's task is to fan the flames of hope and engage the client in a collaborative enterprise to tackle their problems. This may be achieved by following the steps in Table 3.1.

To help reduce the time needed to complete the first interview it is useful to have the client complete a questionnaire beforehand that covers contact details, history of problems, emotional and drink/drug problems, family history and major negative life events. A questionnaire covering the important domains is contained in Appendix B. The open-ended interview begins by asking the client what is the main problem they have been having and encouraging them to elaborate with prompts such as 'tell me more about that'. The therapist can also seek clarification of the completed questionnaire (Appendix B) as a prelude to conducting the 7 Minute Mental Health Screen

Table 3.1 First interview steps

Stage one – diagnostic interview

1. Open-ended interview, establishing rapport
2. The 7 Minute Mental Health Screen or First Step Questionnaire, differential diagnosis
3. Structured interview
4. Diagnoses

Stage two – clinical interview

5. Psychometric tests
6. Sharing of provisional case formulations of each identified disorder
7. Enquiry regarding expectations of therapy
8. Elicitation of negative attitudes regarding self, therapy or therapist
9. Pinpointing most urgent and accessible problems, clarifying goals
10. Define therapist role
11. Define client role to practise mutually agreed strategies between sessions
12. Set homework, where possible, to ensure an immediate experience of success
13. Enquiry regarding reactions to first interview

(Appendix C). For disorders that are highlighted by the screen the therapist then uses a structured interview, Appendix D 'The Cognitive Behaviour Therapy Pocketbook' (or alternatively SCID or ADIS) in order to arrive at diagnoses. To reiterate a point made earlier it is not necessary to cover in one interview all the candidate disorders highlighted by the screen; outstanding possibilities can be examined in detail using the Pocketbook at the next session.

The first interview plays a pivotal role in engaging the client. It is possible in routine clinical practice to be an accomplished cognitive behaviour therapist as measured by the Cognitive Therapy Rating Scale (Young and Beck 1980) (which is designed to rate competence in all sessions except the first) and yet have a high dropout rate after the first session because of a poor first interview. Strangely the structuring of the first interview and assessment of adherence to that structure has become a neglected part of CBT teaching and training, despite Beck *et al.* (1979) specifying a protocol for the first interview and assessment.

Beck's (1979) recommendation is that 1–1.5 hours is scheduled for the first appointment. A relatively long session is needed not only to make significant inroads on the diagnostic assessment but also to reach a point at the end of the interview that the client can be given a strategy that if implemented, offers hope of making some difference before the next session. The duration of the first interview can seem onerous given the pressure of waiting lists, but there is an implicit communication in such a long session, which is 'I really do have time to listen and try and understand you'. This message coming at the beginning of treatment helps offset the typical ambivalence with which clients come to therapy, fostering engagement. The steps to be taken in conducting the first interview are summarised in Table 3.1 and elaborated below.

Stage one – diagnostic interview

1. Open-ended interview and establishing rapport

The therapist has to put the client at ease from the outset: apologising if he/she has been running late, giving the client the option of having any accompanying family member/friend sit in with them during the appointment, making small talk about the weather or difficulties in parking.

It is useful to start the open-ended interview by thanking the client for the completed questionnaire before proceeding to review their description of their main current problems and then asking whether there are any other problems than those already focused upon. In this way the client's goals for therapy can be distilled.

The questionnaire will likely highlight any predisposing factors, such as previous mental health problems, family psychiatric history. When a client has a long psychiatric history or is discursive it is useful to create a time-line with four columns headed age, event, symptoms, treatment to avoid getting lost. As part of clarifying the client's history the therapist should seek elaboration of any possible precipitating events, e.g. break-up of marriage, for current difficulties.

2. The 7 Minute Mental Health Screen or First Step Questionnaire, differential diagnosis

After the open-ended interview the therapist conducts the 7 Minute Mental Health Screen in Appendix C. During this brief interview the therapist not only screens for the presence of each disorder, but also gauges the motivation of the client by asking with regard to highlighted disorders whether this is something that they want help with. Thus there is an inherent consumer view in the screen. The screen in conjunction with records/letters will suggest a number of diagnostic possibilities, i.e. a differential diagnosis, and it is broad enough to ensure that no common mental disorder is missed. Alternatively the client can be asked to complete the First Step Questionnaire (Appendix H) before or during this interview. (However for those who would wish for a broader screen the Psychiatric Diagnostic Screening Questionnaire (Zimmerman and Mattia 2001) can be used and is available from Western Psychological Services (www.wspublish.com); it asks questions about each of the symptoms in 13 DSM-IV disorders, the respondent indicates 'yes' or 'no' with regard to each symptom, cut-offs are provided for each of the disorders, and it takes clients about 20 minutes to complete.)

It is tempting to save time by stopping at the first probable diagnosis. However, it should be borne in mind that co-morbidity is the rule rather than the exception and consideration should be given to alternative and additional diagnoses. Although in a significant minority of cases just one diagnosis suffices, at the differential diagnosis stage there is usually at least one other possible candidate. Very occasionally a disorder does not suggest itself until some way into therapy.

The anxiety algorithm in the previous chapter (Table 2.6) is an aid to differential diagnosis. For example, step 2 of this algorithm recognises that panic attacks are a feature of many anxiety disorders; however, by following the algorithm through specific anxiety disorders can be identified. Thus if a client's panic attacks only occurred when the client was exposed to public scrutiny a diagnosis of social phobia could be confirmed using the social phobia module of the Pocketbook (Appendix D).

3. Structured interview

A structured interview involves directly accessing each symptom in a DSM-IV-TR criteria set for the disorder under consideration, with one or more questions. The Pocketbook in Appendix D provide sets of questions for use.

However, the Pocketbook is not intended for use as a checklist, i.e. a symptom is not endorsed as present simply because the client makes an affirmative response to a question. Whether a symptom is regarded as present is based on all the information available that is pertinent to the question asked, including the client's response to the question. Thus a client may deny being depressed and down most of the day but at interview appeared very glum throughout and if in addition their accompanying partner said 'he just sits there with a face on him all day', the first item on the depression criteria would be endorsed. In order to declare the presence of a symptom it is usually necessary that that symptom produces clinically significant impairment; thus in the example above the first depression symptom would be regarded as present because judging by the tone of the partner's comments it was affecting their relationship. The inter-rater reliability of the Pocketbook is unknown and for research purposes the SCID (First *et al.* 1997), which has an established reliability, would be preferred, but the Pocketbook is sufficient for routine clinical use.

The structured interview should not be conducted like an interrogation with a rapid fire of questions, in which clients are cut short in their reply. It is crucial that clients are given the space and respect to explain themselves. However, it is not at all uncommon for a therapist to conclude, largely on the basis of a client's response to a question, that a particular symptom is not present, then later in the interview apropos of a totally different question to elicit information that suggests that the original symptom is present after all. Conducting a structured interview involves a painstaking teasing out of symptoms rather than rushing through an interview checklist.

It is important when using a structured interview to be clear about the time frame that is being used. The DSM-IV criteria assess for the simultaneous presence of symptoms; thus a client may have suffered at some point from all the symptoms of a disorder but currently though there are some symptoms that are insufficient to meet diagnostic criteria for the disorder, but they perhaps have a 'sub-threshold' level of the disorder. For example, a client may have met criteria for depression in the past but currently is feeling a little better and only has four DSM-IV depression symptoms as opposed to the required five or more symptoms necessary to meet diagnostic criteria for the condition. In such instances CBT would be still appropriate but would be focused on preventing relapse and would likely involve fewer sessions than for a client currently meeting the full criteria.

4. Diagnoses

Whilst every effort should be made to make reliable diagnoses in the first interview, such diagnoses should not be set in stone, but reviewed in the light of any new information. It may for example not be until a partner or relative attends a therapy session that it emerges that the client has rather more of a drink/drug problem than you were led to believe or the informant tells you of the client's gambling problem. This highlights that information from multiple sources helps to make for the most reliable diagnoses. Young males, particularly adolescents, are prone to minimise their symptoms and it is particularly important to get input from others on their functioning.

Though a therapist may identify a number of disorders, they may think in a particular case that one disorder say social phobia is primary and another disorder say depression secondary, because the depression did not develop until some time after the social phobia (the depression representing the consequences of social withdrawal). It is tempting then to think in such an instance that if the social phobia is tackled then the depression will take care of itself. Whilst it is certainly the case that treating one disorder can lead to the resolution of an untargeted disorder, this is not guaranteed. In the author's view it is safer to target usually simultaneously each identified disorder. This does also have the benefit of the client feeling that the totality of their experience is being acknowledged, thereby fostering engagement. There are, however, some important exceptions to tackling disorders simultaneously; if the client has an alcohol/drug problem the other disorders cannot be easily addressed whilst the client is under the influence of these substances. The symptoms of withdrawal from alcohol mimic those of anxiety disorders and it is important not to confuse the two. Generally a substance abuser should be free of direct withdrawal symptoms within a month.

Sufficient information should be gleaned in the diagnostic stage to enable completion of a reliable risk assessment, quantified using the SAD PERSONS Scale (Miller and Giordano 2007) detailed in Chapter 1, Table 1.2. Further, the information from the diagnostic stage should be sufficient to assess the client's overall functioning using the Global Assessment of Functioning Scale (DSM-IV-TR, American Psychiatric Association 2000) detailed in Chapter 1, Table 1.3.

Beck et al. (1979: 79) highlighted the importance of diagnosis thus: 'it is obvious that the therapist should conduct a complete diagnostic evaluation of the patient unless a very thorough diagnostic workup has been conducted prior to the referral to the therapist'; regrettably this is not obvious at all to most current CBT practitioners. It is rare indeed to receive a referral based on a structured interview or to see in CBT practitioner's notes any evidence that a structured interview has been employed.

Stage two – clinical interview

5. Psychometric tests

Psychometric tests are used to gauge the severity of a disorder and to gauge the progress of a client in therapy. The tests can also furnish information of direct relevance to treatment; for example, question 9 on the Patient

Health Questionnaire (PHQ-9, freely available from www.pfizer.com/phq-9) for depression asks client how often over the previous 2 weeks they have been bothered by thoughts that they would be better off dead or of hurting themselves in some way. If a client endorsed such an item there would be a need for detailed enquiry and a challenging of the sense of hopelessness to reduce suicidal risk. Scores of 5, 10, 15 and 20 on the PHQ-9 (Kroenke *et al.* 2001) represent cutpoints for mild, moderate, moderately severe and severe depression, respectively, and can be used as benchmarks for a client's progress in therapy. Indeed the PHQ-9 is so brief that depressed clients can be asked to complete it for homework after each session without any sense of overburdening them, adjusting the time frame to the past week for weekly sessions.

The tests can also highlight key cognitions and behaviour that are perpetuating disorders and become thereby a target for therapeutic intervention.

Some useful psychometric tests for specific disorders are listed in Table 3.2, but the list is not intended to be exhaustive. For each disorder Table 3.2 lists first an instrument that measures the severity of the disorder and then an instrument that taps cognitions thought to play a role in the maintenance of the disorder.

The different scales in Table 3.2 are discussed in detail in the relevant disorder-specific chapters.

6. Sharing of provisional case formulations of each identified disorder

When a client comes to therapy they furnish the story of their difficulties; the therapeutic task is to help them elaborate the full autobiography to date. Unless clients are specifically asked about potential predisposing factors such

Table 3.2 Commonly used tests

1. Depression – Beck Depression Inventory (BDI II, Beck *et al.* 1996), Dysfunctional Attitude Scale (Weissman and Beck 1978)

2. Panic disorder and agoraphobia – Beck Anxiety Inventory (BAI, Beck and Steer 1993), Agoraphobic Cognitions Questionnaire (ACQ, Chambless *et al.* 1984)

3. Post-traumatic Stress Disorder – the PTSD Checklist (PCL, Weathers *et al.* 1993), Posttraumatic Cognitions Inventory (PCTI, Foa *et al.* 1999)

4. Generalised anxiety disorder – GAD-7 Scale (Spitzer *et al.* 2006), Anxious Thoughts Inventory (AnTI, Wells 1994)

5. Social phobia – Social Phobia Inventory (SPIN, Connor *et al.* 2000), Social Cognitions Questionnaire (SCQ, Wells *et al.* 1993)

6. Obsessive Compulsive Disorder – Yale-Brown Obsessive-Compulsive Disorder Inventory (Y-BOCS, Goodman *et al.* 1989), Obsessive Belief Questionnaire (OBQ, Obsessive Compulsive Cognitions Working Group 2005)

as physical or sexual abuse in childhood these are unlikely to be volunteered. Yet how they coped with such early events may well have a bearing on current difficulties. For example, one client called Graham with OCD and depression reported that his 'mother was an alcoholic, she physically abused me, I had to look after my younger brother, I had to just get on with things'. Thus the seeds of Graham's difficulties (the predisposing factors) were likely to be in an excessive sense of responsibility and emotional avoidance (avoiding carefully inspecting what was upsetting him). However, given his background Graham had done extremely well to set up his own motorcycle repair business with his brother, which had worked well for many years (thus a protective factor for Graham was his determination and perseverance). Unfortunately Graham's brother was involved in a motorcycle accident and was unable to work. Graham became overwhelmed by the workload (precipitating factor for OCD) and began repeatedly checking that he had safely done repairs, then repeatedly checking he had locked his door at home and his car door. Graham became unable to pay his brother (precipitating factor for depression) and became depressed. From a cognitive behavioural perspective his OCD was maintained (perpetuating factor) by the immediate relief he felt on checking on things 'once more' and his depression maintained (perpetuating factor) by no longer doing the activities he enjoyed such as going out with fellow bikers at weekends. In constructing a case formulation the therapist is in essence ghost writing the client's autobiography on the basis of the information furnished but structuring it to make clear what are predisposing factors, precipitating factors, perpetuating factors and protective factors. Following the maxim that a 'picture is worth a thousand words', it is helpful to draw the case formulation with the client; thus a diagrammatic representation of Graham's difficulties would look like Figure 3.1.

The bottom of Figure 3.1 shows that when Graham is depressed this affects his OCD and he checks more and further his mood is lowered by his OCD, i.e. the identified disorders reciprocally interact. Summarising a client's history verbally and diagrammatically is the essence of a case formulation and a necessary prelude to being able to construct with the client the next chapter of their autobiography.

7. Enquiry regarding expectations of therapy

Clients come to therapy with a wide range of expectations from an unwarranted pessimism to over-optimism. The therapeutic task is to simultaneously generate hope but avoid unreasonable expectations. It is important to make the client's expectations about therapy explicit and juxtapose this with the likely prognosis in their case. Based on the Butler review of outcome studies shown in Table 1.1, it can reasonably be stated as a rough rule of thumb that the client is likely to do better than 3 out of 4 similar clients who do not have CBT. But they are likely scarred by the experience they have already had,

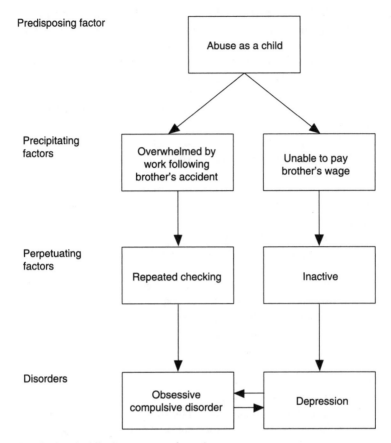

Figure 3.1 Graham's difficulties – a case formulation.

creating a 'fault line' and because of this even after therapy they will need to continue to do special things to avoid cracking along the 'fault line'. It is useful to suggest to the client that they are somewhat a diabetic whose illness is under control provided they follow certain procedures, e.g. not skipping lunch even if they are really busy. The virtue of the diabetic analogy is that it emphasises continuing change of behaviour in order to function very well rather than being cured. The goal within the first interview is to move both the pessimistic and the over-optimistic client to a position of cautious optimism.

8. Elicitation of negative attitudes regarding self, therapy or therapist

Following presentation of the case formulation it is important to get the client's feedback on its accuracy and it may need refining after further discussion with the client. It should be explained that therapy will focus on removing the perpetuating factors and capitalising on protective factors. However, the therapeutic endeavour can be sabotaged by negative attitudes to the self and therapy. Midway through his first interview Graham, whom we met earlier (see Fig. 3.1), had the following dialogue with his therapist:

GRAHAM: I can't see how therapy is going to help, if you can't help yourself who can?

THERAPIST: You have certainly been very good at helping yourself, you ensured you and your brother survived against the odds and built the business.

GRAHAM: A lot of good that did me, here I am seeing a 'shrink'.

THERAPIST: What would have happened to your brother if you had not taken him under your wing?

GRAHAM: It doesn't bear thinking about.

THERAPIST: Sounds like you made a difference?

GRAHAM: Hmm, I guess so.

THERAPIST: I am not at all mechanically minded, if I had something wrong with a motorcycle I guess I would probably take it to a specialist garage, like yours. What is the difference between me doing that and you coming to see me with your difficulties?

GRAHAM: I can see where you're coming from.

In this exchange the therapist has challenged the client's compulsive self-reliance and negative view of self that together were likely to sabotage the development of a therapeutic alliance. The therapeutic challenges have been made using Socratic dialogue, questioning rather than lecturing.

9. Pinpointing most urgent and accessible problems, clarifying goals

Clients come to therapy usually with a plethora of problems. Though the case formulation highlights what is perpetuating their underlying problems and what needs tackling long term, there are often more immediate problems which for the sake of cementing a therapeutic alliance need addressing. Early success on some accessible problems generates hope.

GRAHAM: The tax bill will be due soon, I won't manage that.

THERAPIST: What does your accountant say?

GRAHAM: I've stopped answering letters and returning phone calls.

THERAPIST: Why?

GRAHAM: I just don't want to be bothered with anything.

THERAPIST: What would happen if you contacted your accountant?

GRAHAM: Don't get me wrong he's a good guy.

THERAPIST: Would he be able to talk to the tax people so that the tax isn't based on the income the year before your brother's accident but takes into account the recent great drop in income?

GRAHAM: Can they do that?

THERAPIST: I think so, but I am not sure, you would probably need to have a word with your accountant.

GRAHAM: I've been putting it off, I will call in at the accountant's on the way home.

In this exchange from the outset the therapist is entering into the client's world but the strategies negotiated are in keeping with the long-term therapeutic goals, one of which for Graham was to become active.

The goals of therapy should reflect the client's values, what they think is most important to them at the end of the day. Often what they value is submerged in the current difficulties as illustrated by the following:

THERAPIST: What is most important to you?

GRAHAM: Sorting out this financial mess.

THERAPIST: What is it about sorting out these financial difficulties that is so important?

GRAHAM: Well I've got to provide for my wife, kids and brother.

THERAPIST: Do they think you have to provide to the extent you have done or just do your best?

GRAHAM: No they are not on my back, but obviously they would like more.

THERAPIST: What do they think of you?

GRAHAM: They know I will always be there for them.

THERAPIST: Which is more important providing or being there for them?

GRAHAM: You can't take your money with you, it's family that matters.

The goals in therapy should have the characteristics of the 'SMART' mnemonic in Table 3.3.

In the light of his values and 'SMART', Graham set a specific goal of spending more time with his children and wife, it was measurable in that he wanted to be home from work at least 30 minutes before the children's bedtime and he set the further measurable goal of going out with his biker friends on a Sunday. However, when the therapist asked whether going out each

Table 3.3 Therapeutic goals – 'SMART'

- **S**pecific
- **M**easurable
- **A**chievable
- **R**ealistic
- And have a **T**ime frame

Sunday with friends was achievable given the demands of young children, he agreed this was probably unrealistic but thought that perhaps going out with the bikers one Sunday a month was possibly achievable. He thought the time frame for realising these goals might be about 6 weeks, given the reorganisation at home and work that would be needed.

10. Define therapist role

The therapist has to define his/her role in such a way as to emphasise the collaborative nature of CBT. Understandably some clients bring to therapy the passive role they might assume in a medical consultation, expecting to be simply made better. The therapist has to emphasise the need for the client's active participation. In this connection the therapist can liken his/her role to that of a driving instructor and the client's role to that of a pupil. 'Passing the driving test' will depend as much on the client's practice between sessions as on the therapist's instruction. Continuing the analogy the therapist can stress that like driving lessons progress in therapy is inevitably two steps forward and one back, so that setbacks are budgeted for from the outset.

11. Define client role to practise mutually agreed strategies between sessions

If a therapist defines their role as that of a psychological driving instructor, the way is paved to ask clients to perform certain tasks between sessions. However, these tasks must be mutually agreed. Clients will not engage in these tasks if they have low self-efficacy, i.e. they believe either that the tasks will make no significant difference or they do not believe that they have the capacity to perform the task. Thus the therapist has to address self-efficacy issues from the outset.

THERAPIST: How would you feel if before the next session you only checked you had locked your front door once before leaving for work of a morning?

GRAHAM: I couldn't, I would be so distracted in work that I would just have to go home and check.

THERAPIST: If someone had a gun to your head to stop you going home to check, would that stop you?

GRAHAM: Yes.

THERAPIST: So you could not go back?

GRAHAM: I suppose so, but it would be difficult.

THERAPIST: Is it worthwhile getting you to stop the checking of the front door?

GRAHAM: Oh yes, I must lose at least 20 minutes at the beginning of every working day because of it.

It is very easy to be too busy to check out with clients the perceived viability of an identified homework task but not to do so leads to the non-completion of homework, lack of progress and a souring of the therapeutic relationship.

12. Set homework, where possible, to ensure an immediate experience of success

Whilst therapist competence (as measured by the Cognitive Therapy Rating Scale) has been found to relate to outcome in cognitive therapy for depression (Shaw *et al.* 1999), the effect is modest, accounting for just 19% of the variance in outcome on a clinician-administered measure and with no relation with self-report outcome measures. Further the aspect of competence that was most associated with outcome was structure (this referred to setting an agenda, assigning relevant homework and pacing the session appropriately); by contrast general therapeutic skills or specific CBT skills did not predict outcome. It is not clear whether there would be similar findings for other disorders. It could be that the Cognitive Therapy Rating Scale is a poor measure of competence, nevertheless the CTRS in its original or updated form tends to be the 'gold standard' for assessing CBT students and practitioners across the range of common mental health disorders. The Shaw *et al.* (1999) study should at least caution against an overemphasis on skill at the expense of structure – setting a homework task at the end of sessions (including the first) would seem of key importance. The Therapist Competence Screen (Appendix G) flags up the salience of homework.

Clients arrive at therapy bereft of any recent successes; setting a homework task that conforms with 'SMART' but with an almost immediate time frame can do much to bolster a client's self-esteem and engage them in therapy. The tasks are negotiated in the first interview thus:

THERAPIST: What could you realistically do between now and the next session that would likely give you a sense of achievement?

GRAHAM: Not to be miserable.

THERAPIST: Do you think that is realistic?

GRAHAM: No.

THERAPIST: What else could you try?

GRAHAM: I suppose I could ring my sister, I've not been in contact with her since all this started.

THERAPIST: OK, let's go for that.

Given the importance of homework it is regrettable that in practice CBT practitioners' notes rarely contain a copy of a homework assignment given to a client that in any way conforms to 'SMART'. Usually the notes make at best a general reference to a topic such as 'relaxation tape given' or 'activity scheduling', leaving doubts as to the clarity of what the client is being asked to do. Homework and review of homework provides a continuity between sessions, and it is difficult to see how this is achieved if there is not in 'SMART' terms a very specific record of homework given. Distilling a written homework assignment should involve a practical synthesis of issues addressed and relevant cognitive behavioural strategies in a language that is understandable to the client. The homework is a summary of the session and a highlighting of the practical implications. In asking a client whether the proposed written homework assignment is understandable and relevant the therapist is in effect asking the client for feedback on the session. From an audit point of view there can be no certainty that one of the most important features of CBT, homework, is being competently addressed, without a copy of what instructions were actually given to the client regarding homework. Given clients' typical poor concentration and levels of emotional arousal it is unlikely that they will remember in any detail largely verbal instructions. In the absence of detailed written homework it is difficult for the next session to have a sharp focus on the homework.

There are a variety of means of ensuring the therapist keeps a record of homework given; using a duplicate book with a carbon in it or photocopying the homework are likely to be the most practical. However, the author has found it invaluable to use a Tablet PC, which will automatically print off the homework that the therapist has prepared for the client as well as retaining an electronic copy. This means that near the beginning of the next session it is very easy to review the homework and even to print off another copy if the client has mislaid it. It is of course possible to utilise the handwriting recognition facility on a Tablet PC as well and get a typewritten printed copy of the homework but this does depend on the quality of your handwriting; alas the author's is so poor that he believes it is beyond the wit of any machine ever to do this!

13. Enquiry regarding reactions to first interview

At the end of the first session the therapist should seek feedback about the global impact of the session. Although a client may have been attentive throughout the appointment, appreciating the care with which symptoms were elicited and oftentimes appreciating their relevance for the first time, then agreeing with the case formulation, this is not a guarantee that they will return for the next session. The very simplicity of cognitive behavioural explanations of a client's difficulties occasionally makes some clients think the session has just proved that they are as 'stupid' as they thought and that there is really no point in continuing. The therapist could prevent such a client defaulting thus:

GRAHAM: You have just shown me how stupid I've been, I cock everything up so I am bound to make a mess of this.

THERAPIST: I don't think you will, but you clearly think you will, neither of us has a crystal ball or knows for sure; why not do an experiment, attend at least a few sessions and then make a judgement?

GRAHAM: I could do I suppose.

THERAPIST: Do you have to call yourself 'stupid' just because you got something wrong?

GRAHAM: I don't call the apprentice 'stupid' when he gets it wrong, I hate put downs, it is what my mother did to make herself feel better.

THERAPIST: So you have one law for other people about not putting them down and another for yourself?

GRAHAM: Hmmm, yes, I'll see the sessions through.

In this extract rather than get into an argument with the client about whether or not he will 'mess up' the sessions the therapist has suggested a behavioural experiment to test out the rival predictions; such experiments are an expression of what Beck *et al.* (1979) have termed 'collaborative empiricism'. The therapist has also begun to counter the client's low self-esteem which is so pervasive that unchecked it could sabotage the whole programme.

Each of the disorder-specific chapters will be organised into four parts:

1   Assessment, particular co-morbidities, goal setting and presentation of shared story of the disorder.
2   Case formulation – an individual example of the CBT model of the disorder. A 'Sat Nav' in the form of a table to remind the therapist of the therapeutic targets/destinations and appropriate routes.
3   Session by session programme outline.
4   Focus on modifying the thoughts, beliefs and behaviours operating in the case formulation/story.

In addition, each disorder-specific chapter will be illustrated by following a particular client as a case example.

Chapter 4

Depression

Depression has been termed the 'common cold' of mental health but this can belie its seriousness with approximately 1 in 333 of those prescribed anti-depressants in primary care making a suicide attempt in a 9-month period, with a corresponding figure of 1 in 129 for those starting psychotherapy (Simons and Savarino 2007). Depression affects 9% of individuals over the age of 18 in any given year and approximately 16% of adults will experience depression in their lifetime (Kessler *et al.* 2003). Unfortunately it tends to be a recurring condition with the average sufferer experiencing four life-time episodes of 20 weeks duration (Solomon *et al.* 2001). Depression is the most commonly encountered disorder among psychiatric outpatients (45%), but only 31% of depression sufferers are suffering from depression alone (Zimmerman *et al.* 2008). Table 4.1 shows the pattern of depression co-morbidity.

From Table 4.1 it can be seen that the commonest co-morbidities are PTSD and panic disorder and the least common is obsessive compulsive disorder. Clients have been found to want treatment not only for their principal diagnosis, i.e. the main reason they were seeking treatment, but also for their additional disorders (Zimmerman and Mattia 2000). Thus though the focus of this chapter is on a principal diagnosis of depression, it is intended that treatment take place simultaneously for any of the additional disorders that might be present and whose treatment is described in other chapters in this volume. Thus for example if a client had a diagnosis of depression and

Table 4.1 Depression co-morbidity

No co-morbidity	31%
Panic disorder	38%
Panic disorder with agoraphobia	42%
Social phobia	31%
PTSD	56%
Generalised anxiety disorder	22%
Obsessive compulsive disorder	19%

panic disorder, the therapist should set and review homework pertinent to both disorders.

Diagnosis

DSM-IV-TR (American Psychiatric Association 2000) indicates that a necessary first step in the diagnosis of depression is that the client must have been depressed and down most of the day for more than half the days in the past 2 weeks and/or have lost interest or pleasure in things they usually enjoyed. Questions 1 and 2 respectively in the 7 Minute Health Screen (Appendix C), The First Step Questionnaire (Appendix H) and the Pocketbook (depression section), Appendix D refer to these gateway concerns. The therapist must determine on the basis of all the questions and all the information available whether the client has in total at least five of the symptoms. However, from a clinical point of view if a client had just one too few symptoms to meet the DSM criteria, consideration may still be given to embarking on the programme outlined in this chapter. It is possible that a client could have recovered from a depressive episode and have just three of the DSM depression symptoms. In such an instance the appropriate intervention may be to focus simply on the relapse prevention aspects of the programme.

Beck's model of depression

Beck's model of depression (Beck *et al.* 1979) has led to the development of the most widely evaluated treatment of depression, cognitive therapy. It was later reformulated by Beck (1987) to take better account of the social dimension to depression. The model is summarised in Figure 4.1.

Beck's model (Fig. 4.1) suggests that if some aspect of a person's early environment is 'toxic', e.g. having an unreliable and abusive father, this increases vulnerability to emotional disorder compared to a person in a 'benign' environment. Specifically exposure to such a 'toxic' environment will likely produce a negative cognitive structure or schema in which the individual may think of themselves as unlovable, their personal world as dangerous and their future uncertain. However, not every individual exposed to such a 'toxic' environment would develop a negative schema; whether they would do so would also in part depend on their genetic endowment. (For example, Colman *et al.* (2007) found that heavier babies had lower likelihood of depressive and anxious symptoms throughout their life, whereas delay in first standing and walking was associated with subsequent higher likelihood of symptoms over the life course, controlling for social circumstances and stressful life events during childhood.)

Beck postulated that it is not the negative schema per se that ushers in depression, it is simply a predisposing factor; a precipitating factor in the shape of a pertinent critical incident or incidents is necessary to ignite the

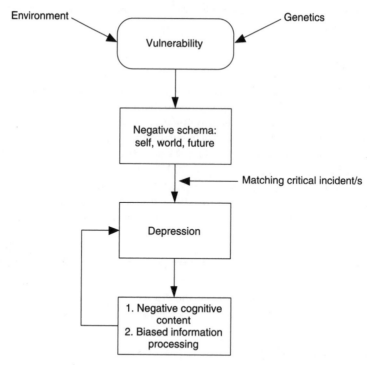

Figure 4.1 Beck's model of depression.

depression. He suggested that the precipitant must match the negative schema (a key and a lock) for the door to be opened to depression. Thus a person whose negative schema contains a belief 'I am unlovable' may suffer no ill effects emotionally if they continue to be in very supportive relationships. Though they are what Beck has termed a sociotrope, addicted to approval, they do not suffer from depression until an important close relationship breaks down (precipitating factor/critical incident). If the sociotrope encountered another critical incident, e.g. failing to get a promotion, this would not usher in depression because achievement is not central to their sense of self-worth. Beck has termed individuals whose sense of worth is based on achievements as 'autonomous' individuals and such a person would be unlikely to suffer depression following say the break-up of a relationship but may well do so if they failed an important exam. There are varying degrees of vulnerability and for one person just one matching precipitant event might be required for them to become depressed but for a less vulnerable person it may require a number of critical incidents. For example, a sociotrope might not succumb to depression simply if their relationship with their partner broke up but might do so if in addition their relationship with their teenage daughter deteriorated. The critical incidents may stack up like water filling a bucket, eventually exceeding the person's resources and overflowing, and the person is swept away on a tidal wave of depression.

The bottom box in Figure 4.1 indicates the factors that serve to perpetuate the depression. Once depressed a negative slant (negative cognitive content) is placed on everyday events. Thus if a depressed employee is told that his boss wants to see him after lunch, he may have no appetite for his lunch, convinced that his boss is going to tell him off. If it transpired that his boss simply wanted to discuss holiday arrangements, the depressive would not conclude that he seems to be automatically looking through the wrong end of the binoculars at everything, rather that he has been lucky on this occasion to have escaped a reprimand. But it is not just the content of the depressive's thinking that serves to perpetuate the depression, there is also faulty information processing. Beck (1967) originally identified six information processing biases, but Burns (1999) has broken these down further to create the list of ten shown in Table 4.2

There are no water-tight distinctions between the information processing biases and many depressed clients customarily use a number of them.

In a further refinement of Beck's model that again emphasises the social dimension of depression, Champion and Power (1995) suggest that one of the critical incidents that can precipitate depression is the loss of a valued role or goal. Further they postulate that the individual is especially vulnerable if

Table 4.2 Information processing biases

1. Dichotomous (black and white) thinking, e.g. 'I'm either a total success or a failure'.
2. Mental filter, focusing on the negative to the exclusion of the positive, e.g. 'how can you say it was a lovely meal, how long did we have to wait for the dessert to be served?'
3. Personalisation, assuming just because something has gone wrong it must be your fault, e.g. 'John did not let on to me coming into work this morning, must have been something I said'.
4. Emotional reasoning, assuming guilt simply because of the presence of guilt feelings, e.g. 'I can't provide for the kids the way I did, I've let them down, what sort of parent am I?'
5. Jumping to conclusions, e.g. assuming that being asked to have a word with your line manager means that you are in trouble.
6. Overgeneralisation, making negative predictions on the basis of one bad experience, e.g. 'I've had it with men after Charlie, you cannot trust any of them'.
7. Magnification and minimisation, magnifying faults or difficulties and minimising strengths or positives, e.g. 'I am terrible at report writing and I am lucky to have got good appraisals for the last couple of years'.
8. Disqualifying the positives, e.g. brushing aside compliments and dwelling on criticism.
9. Should statements, overuse of moral imperatives, e.g. 'I must do . . ., I should . . ., I have to . . .'.
10. Labelling and mislabelling, e.g. 'if I make a mistake I am a failure as a person'.

prior to the loss they have overvalued the role or goal, using it to totally define their sense of worth.

The summary of Beck's model of depression in Figure 4.1 is not intended to imply that he believes a cognitive account of depression is the only possible perspective, it is equally possible to view depression from a complementary biological perspective. For example, Fales *et al.* (2008) have looked at depressives' enhanced responsiveness to and memory for specific negative memories and found both impaired top-down cognitive control, potentially linked to deficits in dorsolateral prefrontal cortex (a cortical structure), and enhanced bottom-up responses, potentially linked to deficits in amygdala (a subcortical structure) and anterior cingulate functioning.

The cognitive cycle

Whilst the reciprocal interactions of cognitions, behaviour, emotion and physiology are depicted in Figure 1.1, the cognitive cycle in Figure 4.2 provides a more fine-grained illustration of the processes involved. From Figure 4.2 it can also be seen that the social climate in which a person operates can have a

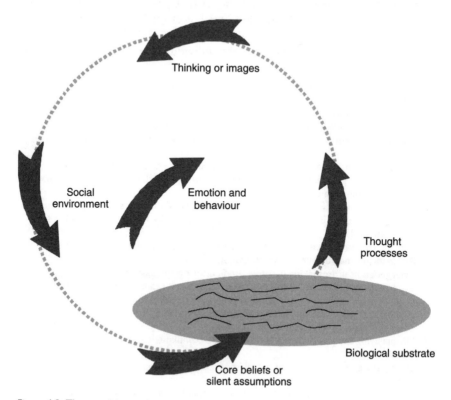

Figure 4.2 The cognitive cycle.

major effect on their emotions. In this connection recovered depressives have been found to be more likely to relapse if subjected to high levels of criticism and/or over-involvement (Hooley *et al.* 1986).

In the cognitive cycle (Fig. 4.2) emotion and behaviour are products of the interaction of the cognitive 'ports', the particular biological substrate involved in the disorder and the social environment in which the person operates. In turn emotion and behaviour affect both the biology and cognitive processing (as well as each other), completing the cycle. (The biological substrate can be further divided between cortical and subcortical structures, the latter reciprocally interacts with the somatic and autonomous nervous systems – not shown in Figure 4.2 for simplicity. Further the cortical and subcortical structures also reciprocally interact.) It is possible in principle to influence emotion via any of the cognitive 'ports'. The cycle in Figure 4.2 indicates that a person could also alter their emotion by exercise or taking antidepressants. It is also possible to replace an emotion with an emotion, e.g. get angry with the boss for shouting, rather than get depressed. For any one individual it is not entirely clear which are going to be ultimately the best routes for influencing emotion. For example, in a study by Beach and O'Leary (1986) of depressed married women, one half were treated with individual cognitive behaviour therapy and one half with marital therapy (principally involving communication training) and the depression lifted equally in both groups. Thus there are probably a number of ways of skinning the depression cat!

Case formulation

A cognitive behavioural case formulation is a specific example of a cognitive model of a disorder. The first step in the case formulation is to determine what disorder or disorders the person is a 'case' of. The next steps are then to specify the precipitants for the disorder(s), identify the predisposing or vulnerability factors, determine the perpetuating factors and finally identify potential springboards or protective factors. The steps to be followed in a case formulation are illustrated with respect to a client, Sarah.

1. Diagnosis   Sarah was referred 12 months after her husband died totally unexpectedly of a brain aneurysm. Following detailed enquiry about each of the symptoms that comprise the DSM-IV criteria set for the disorder (see depression section of Pocketbook, Appendix D) and review of records she was diagnosed as suffering from depression. (A diagnosis of depression is not made for at least 2 months after a bereavement and Sarah's difficulties in those early days would have been regarded as a 'normal' grief reaction; however, their continuance beyond this window constituted a DSM-IV diagnosis of depression.) To gauge the severity of Sarah's depression the Beck Depression Inventory (Beck *et al.* 1996) was administered and her score of 28 indicated moderate depression. As Sarah was a 'case' of depression, the formulation was mapped onto Beck's model in Figure 4.1. Sarah also developed panic attacks and met criteria for panic disorder; this aspect of her difficulties is addressed in the next chapter.

2. Precipitants   Sarah had not returned to nursing since her husband's death and was isolated in the care of her two pre-school children. With regard to Beck's model the precipitating event was the death of her husband.

3. Vulnerability   Sarah had not had her children until her forties, following three miscarriages and a stillbirth; she and her husband had been wanting children for 20 years, and their overriding goal was what Sarah referred to as a 'normal' family life. Of itself this goal evoked no psychopathology, but did constitute a predisposing factor. After the children were born Sarah and her husband were in her view an excellent 'team', managing to integrate the demands of shift work with childcare. By Sarah's account, they both felt they had achieved their goal. However, with the untimely death of her husband Sarah lost her valued goal and became depressed. Sarah's parents were elderly and unable to assist, as were her husband's, and her friends were busy working.

4. Perpetuating factors   A diagnosis indicates the type of negative cognitions; depressogenic cognitions are reflected in the Dysfunctional Attitude Scale (DAS, Weissman and Beck 1978), a 40-item questionnaire designed to assess maladaptive cognitions including concern with evaluation, perfectionistic standards of performance, causal attributions and rigid ideas about the world. Sarah completed the DAS and endorsed the following items 'taking even a small risk is foolish because the loss is likely to be a disaster', 'if a person asks for help, it is a sign of weakness', 'if you cannot do something well, there is little point in doing it at all', 'if I don't set the highest standards for myself, I am likely to end up a second-rate person', 'I should be upset if I make a mistake', 'if you don't have other people to lean on, you are bound to be sad', 'I cannot reach important goals without slave driving myself', 'I cannot be happy if I miss out on many of the good things in life' and 'being isolated from others is bound to lead to unhappiness'. Two main themes emerged from her DAS: a perfectionism and a fixed view of how the world has to be to achieve happiness. Her perfectionism was leading her to exhaust herself, her compulsive self-reliance to a hesitancy about seeking treatment and her exaggerated view about the importance of having a partner was leading to inactivity on her own behalf.

Sarah's depression was maintained not only by negative cognitive content but also by biases in the way in which she processed information. At interview her use of 'magnification and minimisation' (see Table 4.2) was much in evidence; she described herself as having 'no time for myself' but later said her children were at Nursery for two and a half hours of a morning (magnifying her difficulties). Sarah also reported that 'nobody cares' when in fact her parents and friends did try to provide as much support as they were capable of (minimising the positives). She also utilised dichotomous thinking, she exclaimed 'I've been cheated I want my life back again and it is not going to happen', implying the only alternative to life as it was before her husband's death was a nothingness.

Sarah began to experience unexpected panic attacks about 2 months after her husband died and they were ongoing at the time of the assessment and it was concluded that she additionally met criteria for panic disorder. The case formulation of this aspect of Sarah's functioning is described in the next chapter. The depression pre-dated the panic disorder but the latter was helping to perpetuate it.

5. Protective factors   Historically Sarah was a very resilient person, who had coped with a series of miscarriages and a great deal of job stress. At one stage in her career she had had to re-apply for her own position and at another point in her nursing career ended up being a line manager of a person who had held the position previously and been downgraded following disciplinary action. At interview it was clear that Sarah was very prepared to do whatever was necessary to get better, and her determination and commitment augured well for completing homework assignments. Further Sarah did have some social support, albeit that this was emotional rather than practical, and it might be possible to build on this support.

No cognitive model of a disorder could hope to adequately describe every case of a disorder. In the physical world Newton's laws of motion explain everyday phenomena, such as the speed with which one billiard ball will travel if hit by another at a certain speed. However, it transpired that these laws are actually a special 'case' of Einstein's theory of relativity, and a Sat Nav would in fact give erroneous results if it was constructed based on Newtonian physics; rather it is based on the theory of relativity. However, even the theory of relativity cannot explain what happened in the few seconds after the creation of the Universe. In a similar way one cannot expect any cognitive model to be all encompassing; where it 'fails' can be stimulus for the development of a wider model but in the meantime the cognitive behavioural practitioner is best advised to follow a manualised approach.

Depression Sat Nav

The depression Sat Nav in Table 4.3 is intended to help the therapist not stray too far from the effective treatment of the depressed client and give direction when lost. Being at a loss in or before a therapy session is commonplace, albeit that it happens less often with experience, and it is useful to have a reference point at those moments. But the Sat Nav is an aid and not meant to

Table 4.3 Depression Sat Nav

Therapeutic targets	Treatment strategies
1. Depression about depression	Focus on responsibility for working on solutions and not on responsibility for problem
2. Inactivity	Developing a broad investment portfolio, wide-ranging modest investments
3. Negative views of self, personal world and future	Challenging the validity, utility and authority by which these views are held. Use of MOOD chart
4. Information processing biases	Highlighting personal biases and stepping around them using MOOD chart
5. Overvalued roles	Valuing multiple roles, renegotiation of roles in social context
6. Relapse prevention	Personally constructed self-help 'manual', utilising key points from therapy and drawing on self-help books and computer-assisted material

replace the session by session guidance given later. Continuing the analogy, a Sat Nav can only be appropriately used if the person can drive, understands the Highway Code, etc., and in the same way the Sat Nav for a particular disorder is only viable against a background of the session by session guidance for that disorder and possession of CBT skills.

Depression about depression (double depression) is commonplace. At her first interview Sarah said that the previous day she had bumped into an elderly friendly former neighbour who had told her that she was in the process of sorting out funeral arrangements for her daughter. Sarah expressed her condolences, but came away from the encounter angry at herself for 'fussing' over her own current difficulties. The therapist suggested that it was enough for anyone to simply share the bereavement experience with the former neighbour than beat herself up for her feelings of depression. Sarah agreed that it might be more useful to show she cared by attending the funeral service if possible and added that she would have to go to the hairdresser's first, something she rarely did since her husband died. This led on to a discussion of the importance of scheduling into her week potentially uplifting events. At the next therapy session her activity scheduling was reviewed but the therapist felt at a loss when Sarah reported that though she attended the funeral she felt devastated as it brought back memories of her husband's funeral and she felt that 'I made a show of myself'. The therapist glanced at the Sat Nav and decided that at this juncture it would be appropriate to introduce the MOOD thought record (Table 4.4). It was explained that an important way of dealing with upsets is to do a slow motion action replay of the situation and come up with an alternative way of playing/thinking in the situation. In this way dips in mood could be 'mopped' up before the next hassle arrived,

Table 4.4 MOOD thought record

<u>M</u>onitor mood	<u>O</u>bserve thinking	<u>O</u>bjective thinking	<u>D</u>ecide what to do and do it

thereby stopping a downward spiralling of mood as everyday hassles are dealt with inappropriately. 'MOOD' is a mnemonic for helping remember the mood-altering framework in Table 4.4 (reproduced in Appendix E). The first letter 'M' stands for monitoring mood, 'What am I feeling? What Mood am I in?' and 'What effect is it having on others?' It is explained that noticing and understanding the origins of dips in mood is a key aspect of emotional intelligence; without this it is not possible to fine-tune emotions as you go along, so that by the time you are forced to recognise the distress it is much more difficult to do anything about it. The first 'O' stands for observing thinking or images, identified by asking, 'What have I been saying to myself to feel the way I do?' The second 'O' stands for objective thinking – a standing back from an upset and having second thoughts. The second thoughts can be distilled by asking, 'How true is it? How useful is this way of thinking? Would others be looking at this in a different way?' The 'D' stands for deciding to put into practice the more objective way of thinking, thus stopping depressive rumination.

Using the MOOD thought record, Sarah was able to identify her mood as dipping as she saw her ex-neighbour's daughter's coffin being brought into the church; she began to sob and identified with the latter's mother walking behind, but then thought how much more desperate it must be to lose your only child, even if they were an adult. Sarah's observed thinking was that she was 'stupid' for getting so upset because she did not really know the deceased, the latter had left home before she got to know the neighbour. She was embarrassed that a stranger next to her in the pew gave her a hug; this prompted thoughts of her husband and an intense feeling that she wanted him present now. Her sobbing increased and she went outside to compose herself, returning after a few minutes. After the service was over she was able to briefly greet the ex-neighbour and they hugged. To help distil the objective thinking, the therapist asked her by what authority she believed she made a mess of the funeral. Sarah replied that it was what she thought and then asked whether the deceased's mother had the same view. She acknowledged that the ex-neighbour had been delighted to see her and gave her a very warm hug. The therapist then asked which view mattered at the end of the day. Sarah realised that if she had thought more objectively she would have gone on to the reception afterwards (the 'D' of MOOD) instead of going home and brooding on her 'failure'. The therapist also used this incident to illustrate how Sarah used a mental filter, focusing on her distress instead of her positive effect on the deceased's mother. For homework Sarah was set the task of using the MOOD thought record.

Sarah had lost the role of wife and at times she felt the loss very acutely. Given the quality of the relationship she had had with her husband, the therapist suggested that it might be useful to try and think what her husband would be saying at these moments. At the next session she reported back that she could almost hear her husband calling her by his nickname for her and telling her to do different things such as the garden. But she felt that this might be a sign of madness! The therapist suggested analysing this thought using MOOD and asked her how useful it had been to 'hear' her husband, Sarah replied that she had actually done some gardening as a consequence. She was pleasantly startled when the therapist suggested that if something was useful use it. The therapist used this opportunity to suggest the development of a variety of new roles, including gardening, and explained that a broad investment portfolio confers more protection in the end.

Near the end of therapy the therapist suggested that Sarah write her own survival manual of what she had found most important in therapy and what to do when her mood begins to plummet. Sarah wrote that her biggest enemy was sitting brooding, thinking 'it's not fair . . .' but added that she did not just want to 'survive' but be 'alive' and she made a list of activities in which she could lose herself.

The depression Sat Nav is not intended to stand alone, but to be utilised with Sat Navs for other disorders if present and operationalised in the context of session by session guidance for the disorder.

Session by session programme

The procedures to be followed in the first interview have been described in the previous chapter; there now follows a session by session protocol for depression, from session 2 onwards. The programme is based on that described by Beck *et al.* (1979) in their seminal work *Cognitive Therapy of Depression*, updated to include more recent reading material and including just those procedures that have since come to be seen as constituting the active ingredients of the programme.

Second interview

Table 4.5 outlines the second interview.

Directly asking about the effects of the first interview at the beginning of the second interview sometimes reveals more ambivalence on the part of the client than the therapist had appreciated at the first interview. Whilst Sarah reported that she found the first session useful and felt she 'got a lot off my chest', this acknowledgement was followed by her saying 'I should be able to sort it out myself'. The therapist felt that such a belief was producing unnecessary guilt and could potentially lead her to default from therapy and so asked her whether she would expect one of her cardiac patients with unusual cardiac rhythms to sort it out themselves. She replied that of course she wouldn't and then the therapist asked why depression should be any different to cardiac problems. Sarah wasn't totally convinced by this line of questioning but did reply 'I can see where you are coming from' and the therapist then felt that at least the therapeutic alliance was not going to be sabotaged by such a belief.

The rationale for activity scheduling in Table 4.5 arises from Beck's (1987) evolutionary model of depression, in which depression is viewed as an attempt not to squander scarce resources in a hostile environment. In modern parlance it is as if the client is on strike for better pay and conditions and has stopped investing in life. But if there is no investment there can be no return. For homework following the first interview the client is encouraged to invest. The investments between sessions have to

Table 4.5 Second interview

1. Enquiry regarding effect of first interview
2. Review of activity scheduling
3. Review of reactions to reading Chapter 3 of David Burns' book *Feeling Good: The New Mood Therapy* (1999), pp. 28–49, 'Understanding your moods: you feel the way you think'
4. Discussion of problems and accomplishments since previous interview
5. Scheduling of activities until next interview
6. Enquiry to reactions to present interview

involve activities that strike a balance between a sense of achievement and pleasure.

Becoming active is a major hurdle for depressed clients and the therapist has to inoculate the client against failure experiences by scheduling small 'doses' of activity. Clients should be advised that it is difficult in advance to know what dose of activity they can manage at the moment and that the scheduled activity is a 'best guess' that can easily be revised in the light of experience. The therapist should ask in advance whether the client believes they have the capacity to perform the 'dose' of activity planned and whether they believe that dose would make a worthwhile difference, i.e. assess the client's self-efficacy. In conveying an understanding of the client's problems in becoming active, it is useful to use a metaphor, e.g. 'depression is like having a big heavy weight around your neck, to do anything is a major achievement'. Oftentimes clients respond to such a metaphor that they wish their depression was more visible like a 'broken arm' so that others could understand why they are inactive.

Clients can easily feel that there is something odd about them for having to see a therapist. Asking clients at the end of the first interview to read Chapter 3 of Burns' book is a way of normalising therapy for the client. This chapter explains simply the effect of thinking on mood and details the information processing biases. Clients can also dip into other chapters if they so wish, for example about antidepressant medication. Reviewing the client's response to reading Chapter 3 can help the therapist gauge whether the client has grasped the essential point of cognitive therapy that it is largely how one takes a photograph of a situation rather than the situation per se that determines emotional response. The therapist should not be put off further enquiry if the client says they were 'too busy' or 'too lazy' to read the chapter; the reasons for the non-compliance with the homework need distilling. It could be that the client has problems with literacy, in which case rather than disputing automatic negative thoughts as in cognitive therapy the more appropriate approach would be to use Meichenbaum's (1985) self-instruction training in which coping statements for a variety of different situations are rehearsed. Alternatively it could be that the client believes they should just feel better without having to do anything and the therapist would need to stress that success can only be achieved if both therapist and client do their bit.

Third interview

The third interview is outlined in Table 4.6.

At the outset of the session the therapist should negotiate an agenda. Without an agreed structure to the session it is very easy for the session to be totally dominated by the client's over-detailed description of some negative event that has occurred since the last session. Limiting this discourse and

Table 4.6 Third interview

1. Agreeing an agenda
2. Discussion of reaction to previous interview
3. Review of homework
4. Discussion of automatic negative thoughts ('MOOD')
5. Distilling homework
6. Feedback regarding today's session

relating it to the new material to be taught in the session is part of the art of cognitive therapy. The client should be given space to express their pressing concerns and time should be scheduled to address these. In rare instances, for example if the client is suicidal or there has been a death of a close family member, the usual format of the interview will be suspended. The following is an excerpt of the third interview with Sarah:

THERAPIST: How did you get on with the things we agreed you would have a go at last time?

SARAH: Well, I got myself going, visited my ex-neighbour, we are just sat there and there is a huge bang, we rush out, I am in panic, find that there is an ambulance that had hit a wall down the street, it was mayhem, Fire Brigade arrived to cut them out and . . .

THERAPIST: How did your ex-neighbour react?

SARAH: She just said 'you never know the day', too right!

THERAPIST: How do you cope with that uncertainty?

SARAH: I am a worrier always have been, but when husband was alive would just bounce worry off him and would be OK.

THERAPIST: Last time we looked at using the MOOD record to sort out what was bothering you, for homework I suggested using MOOD, how did that work out?

SARAH: I completely forgot about it, it has been so hectic.

THERAPIST: So what did you do instead about your worries?

SARAH: I just went over and over how awful it is going to be financially if I have to give up work.

THERAPIST: Did going over and over it help?

SARAH: No, just made me feel sick.

THERAPIST: So that if picking at the worry isn't useful and you can't bounce it off your husband what else can you do?

SARAH: OK, sorry I should have tried to sort it out using MOOD.

THERAPIST: The old ways of playing things either aren't available or don't work, so it might be useful to conduct an experiment and see if these new ways of playing it make a difference.

SARAH: It seems strange bothering to write down what is bothering you, makes it real.

THERAPIST: I think that when you write it down there is a moment when sight of your first thoughts, the first 'O' – observe thinking takes your breath away, but if you stay with it and come up with second thoughts the second 'O' it usually takes the edge off the distress and importantly you come up with a game plan a 'Do' – the final column of MOOD, which interrupts the depressive rumination. If you can't find credible second thoughts, that is what I get paid for to help you find so don't worry if you can only manage a column or two of MOOD to begin with.

SARAH: It makes it easier to think I am not alone in sorting out MOOD, I will have a go.

THERAPIST: You did in fact do the other item we put down for homework of being more active, visiting the ex-neighbour.

SARAH: Well I did have a panic attack at the 'bang' but I was determined that I'd concentrate on my ex-neighbour, she has been through such a lot.

THERAPIST: I think we should spend a few minutes on the panic attacks and we can work out an approach for you to try out.

SARAH: OK, the attacks do put me off going places but I was glad I went to visit her. I am not just a mum there are other things I can do.

In the above excerpt the therapist does not scold Sarah for not doing her homework but suggests 'collaborative empiricism', an experiment with regard to completion of the MOOD record, rather than argue the case. The therapist also carefully explores possible reasons for non-completion of the assignment and seeks to negate them. Further the therapist encourages Sarah for what she has managed to do. In the setting of homework the therapist is alert to also address the co-morbid disorder, in Sarah's case the panic disorder (the details of which are included in the next chapter).

Fourth interview

The fourth interview is outlined in Table 4.7.

Sometimes the reflex negative automatic thoughts of the client are at the edge of their awareness rather than at the forefront of their mind. If the subject matter relates to a past event, having the client construct a 'slow

Table 4.7 Fourth interview

1. Follow same general format as in third interview
2. Accessing negative automatic thoughts using 'induced fantasy' or role play if necessary
3. Identifying themes amongst negative automatic thoughts – silent assumptions
4. Model the cross-examination of first negative thoughts/silent assumptions by challenging variously their validity, utility and their authority
5. Identifying any saboteurs to the setting of homework

motion action replay' of the situation they had a problem with uncovers the maladaptive cognition. Further if the focus is on a possible forthcoming event, the client can be encouraged to engage in the typical scenario ('fantasy') they believe will unfold and access the likely pivotal negative automatic thoughts. An alternative is to role play the anticipated scene and the therapist then asks the client what they are thinking at the moment he/she detects discomfort. Both the fantasy and role play are ways of making the pertinent negative cognition 'hot' so it is more available than from a simple verbal exercise.

In helping the client discover second thoughts in response to the negative automatic thoughts the therapist should be mindful that some reflex thoughts are more important than others. Most important are the first thoughts that reflect the key silent assumptions or dysfunctional attitudes that play a pivotal role in the person's depression. The therapist's task is to engage the client in Socratic dialogue focusing on the key thoughts and assumptions. The therapeutic style should be closer to that of the TV detective Colombo, juxtaposing contradictory information with bemused befuddlement rather than being interrogatory. However, there are a range of questions (Table 4.8; see Murphy 1985) that can be subsumed under three core questions that can be useful at various points in the interview. The secret is to change the question when one question or line of questioning is not bearing fruit.

In Sarah's case the themes to the dysfunctional schemas, identified by the DAS, related to perfectionism and a fixed view of how the world has to be to achieve happiness. The therapist was therefore particularly alert to expressions of these attitudes and engaged Sarah in a re-examination of them using some of the probes in Table 4.8.

SARAH: Sorry, I'm late, I hate being late, I was about to take the kids to Nursery before coming here, then John decides to pour a blackcurrant drink down his top. I had to change him then I couldn't find a clean top

Table 4.8 Questions for dialogue

1. *How realistic is the silent assumption?*
   i. Is it valid?
   ii. Is it consistent?
   iii. Is it useful?
2. *By what authority is the silent assumption held?*
   i. By a consensus?
   ii. By an expert view?
   iii. By own view?
3. *Does the silent assumption help achieve a desired goal?*
   i. How close is the achievement of the goal?
   ii. Is a change of means necessary to achieve the goal?
   iii. Is another goal more appropriate?

that really went with his shorts, I bundled them in the car, he's crying because I've been cross with him. After I dropped them off at Nursery I felt so guilty, they are without a Dad and I'm shouting at them for nothing, then I couldn't find a parking space here.

THERAPIST: I hadn't noticed that you were late.

SARAH: I suppose it is only 5 minutes.

THERAPIST: I often end up running up to 30 minutes late; how do you react if I'm running late?

SARAH: That's OK, you can't just cut people off in midstream.

THERAPIST: I noticed on the DAS you completed and from what you just said, 'got to be on time, got to get the right top', that you seem to operate on a silent assumption that you have got to do everything perfectly, how does that sound?

SARAH: Well that's right, probably comes from my nurse training, working in A and E, if you don't get it right someone is going to end up dead!

THERAPIST: Do other work colleagues have this perfectionism?

SARAH: We're understaffed in A and E, I know two nurses off on long-term sick because of the pressures, one of them has developed a drink problem and she was such a perfectionist.

THERAPIST: What about staff still there?

SARAH: There is some good banter, one of the consultants is very good and has a motto of what gets done gets done, just prioritise as best you can, he says how long people wait is not his problem.

THERAPIST: So it is your view that you should be a perfectionist, not everybody's in A and E.

SARAH: Well yes I suppose it is mainly me and maybe Marie who is off with a drink problem. But I think the consultant buries his head in the sand.

THERAPIST: How useful is the consultant's way of working?

SARAH: He does keep morale up and you can count on him. If I'm honest part of the fear of a return to work is not only the problems of looking after the kids but also that I'm not going to do a proper job.

THERAPIST: If you borrowed the consultant's way of thinking rather than Marie's would it be easier?

SARAH: Yes.

THERAPIST: How valid is it to apply this perfectionism to everyday things like being late, wearing the right things?

SARAH: I suppose it is a habit more than anything.

THERAPIST: If you had said to yourself this morning that it is a guideline not to be late or for the children to wear the right thing, rather than that they were 11th and 12th Commandments would it have been easier?

SARAH: I don't think I would have taken off on John if I had thought of guidelines, rather than Commandments. It is silly really, I did read about the overuse of the 'Shoulds' in Chapter 3 of the Burns book and thought 'that's me' but I still do it.

THERAPIST: Breaking old habits dies hard, the first step is recognising when you are doing it, in your case the warning sign seems to be irritability, so as soon as you get irritable it is important to use MOOD and check out for perfectionistic first thoughts, then step around them with more objective second thoughts.

SARAH: I guess in most situations, doing things to a good enough level is enough.

THERAPIST: Probably less exhausting.

SARAH: Yes.

THERAPIST: For homework, it might be an idea to use MOOD when you are getting irritable?

SARAH: But it is going to be too late by the time I think of MOOD, I've already gone over the top and they are situations where you can't just sit down with pen and paper.

THERAPIST: I think you are right you do need some space to use MOOD, but you don't necessarily have to have the opportunity to write it down. You could have probably done it in your head driving from Nursery to here and the idea of MOOD is to eventually be able to do it in your head. But I doubt you could have used it in the 'emergency' when John had spilt blackcurrant on him just before leaving home. For these 'emergency' situations you might use a self-instruction training procedure, the first step is to become aware of the first bodily sign of anger. What would that be for you?

SARAH: I think I clench my teeth.

THERAPIST: When you notice the first signs of anger, e.g. the clenched teeth, then come up with a coping image, e.g. visualising a guideline such as the Highway Code alongside Commandments inscribed in tablets of stone, to show at most a guideline has been broken, e.g. children misbehaving. Finally you engage in a coping behaviour, e.g. just dropping your jaw and shoulders and saying relax as you breathe out or if you are beside your-self with anger going into another room until you compose yourself. How would you feel about trying this procedure in 'emergencies'?

SARAH: Sounds good.

THERAPIST: I will write it down on the homework sheet, together with using MOOD for other situations and the strategies we have discussed for the panic attacks (see next chapter). I would also like to do a stocktaking; could you complete and bring along the BDI and DAS to the next session?

SARAH: OK.

In the above extract the therapist has stayed with an immediate experience of the client 'being late' because it was accessing already identified dys-functional attitudes in a vivid ('hot') manner. Then the therapist examined the authority for this perfectionism: was it the client's own view or was it shared by other colleagues? The focus then shifted to the utility of the perfectionism and then to the validity of the perfectionism: was it appropriate in everyday situations? Finally the focus was on whether the perfectionism was helping achieve a desired goal, a return to work. The therapist was also concerned to translate the Socratic dialogue into a specific procedure that would make a difference to the handling of everyday life, but had to carefully negotiate a viable homework assignment and integrate a strategy derived from another member of the cognitive behaviour therapy family, self-instruction training (Meichenbaum 1985). Finally the therapist has arranged for a mid-therapy stocktaking.

Fifth interview

The fifth interview is outlined in Table 4.9.

The therapist begins the session, as always suggesting the items he/she would like to put on the agenda and asking the client what issues they would like to schedule in. Without a mid-therapy stocktaking it is very easy to forget about some issues that though flagged up at the initial interviews have not been systematically focused on. Re-administration of the psychometric tests and the determination of current diagnostic status using a structured interview can provide a re-focusing of therapy as follows:

THERAPIST: Thanks for completing the BDI and DAS again. On the BDI, you scored 21, previously you scored 28, a change of 7 is regarded as a clinically significant improvement, how does it feel to you?

SARAH: I'm certainly better, but I do have my moments.

THERAPIST: I would just like to check that out, using some of the questions I asked in the first interview, if that's OK?

SARAH: Sure.

Table 4.9 Fifth interview

---

1. Follow same general format as in previous interview
2. Mid-therapy stocktaking
3. Review investment portfolio, broad enough to include primarily achievement investments and primarily pleasure investments
4. Review dips in mood using MOOD
5. Ask the client when using the MOOD thought record, to remind themselves that they have three tools available with which to challenge the negative automatic thought: 'how true is this thought?', 'how useful is this thought?' and 'is it just me who thinks this way in this situation? Could I borrow someone else's way of thinking in this situation?' In this way they can distil objective thinking (column three of MOOD)
6. Explain the role of a behavioural experiment as a fourth tool with which to challenge a negative automatic thought, by seeing the latter as just a 'thought', not a reality. The 'truth' or otherwise of the negative automatic thought to be demonstrated by an experiment

---

THERAPIST: How many days in the last 2 weeks have you felt depressed and down most of the day?

SARAH: Probably 2 or 3 days a week now.

THERAPIST: What goes over in your mind on those days?

SARAH: I just go over what life would have been like if Mark hadn't died.

THERAPIST: You don't think life could be good again?

SARAH: I can't see it.

THERAPIST: I noticed on the DAS that though your attitudes are less perfectionist you still believe that life has to be a certain way in order to be good. We haven't looked at these ideas yet; maybe we could begin focusing on them today, how would that be?

SARAH: OK.

THERAPIST: How are you now with interest and pleasure in the things you used to do before Mark's death.

SARAH: I'm getting better, I'm wanting to do things more like go to the hairdresser's, though I fear having a panic attack sitting so long under the dryer, and I enjoy visiting the old neighbour. I've even enjoyed reading for a few minutes, with a cup of tea immediately after dropping the kids off at Nursery.

THERAPIST: How often are the unexpected panic attacks?

SARAH: I've had only one bad one in the last 2 weeks.

THERAPIST: I think that you are no longer clinically depressed, in that you are not depressed and down most of the day for more than half the days in the week and there is enjoyment of activities, but there are still some depression symptoms. We are certainly moving in the right direction but there is a bit more work to do on the depression and the panic disorder.

SARAH: Yes, I'm getting there.

In the above extract the therapist has noted an improvement in Sarah's condition in that she no longer meets either of the two DSM-IV gateway symptom criteria for depression and this is reflected in a change in BDI score, but there are still days of prolonged depressed mood and the panic disorder persists. Further the DAS has reminded the therapist of a neglected issue, the client's fixed view of how the world ought to be in order to be happy. In the following extract the therapist helps the client re-examine her fixed view of the world:

THERAPIST: You seem to have made some improvement in your mood by what you do, for example by visiting your ex-neighbour, doing a little reading.

SARAH: Yes.

THERAPIST: Is it absolutely necessary to have a partner to become at least just reasonably content?

SARAH: I suppose not, but I miss Mark so!

THERAPIST: What do you imagine Mark would be saying to you now?

SARAH (smiling): Probably something stupid like, 'I'm just incredible, you are bound to miss me', he wasn't much given to humility!

THERAPIST: What would he be saying to you to do?

SARAH: 'Just dance, get on with things'.

THERAPIST: Would that make a difference?

SARAH: I suppose it could, it's just trusting that the 'dancing' will deliver.

THERAPIST: Is it worth the experiment?

SARAH: Yes.

THERAPIST: How true is it that you have got to be in a relationship?

SARAH: Well my ex-neighbour lost her husband long before I ever met her and she just got on with things. But everyone is different.

THERAPIST: That might in part be because some choose to cast all their votes for 'dancing' and some choose not to?

SARAH: It is going to be difficult but I will try.

In the above exchange the therapist has helped the client re-examine her core belief about the conditions necessary for happiness by shifting the focus of authority (see Table 4.8) from the client herself to that of her esteemed deceased husband. At the same time the therapist is not denying the pain of the loss. Further the therapist does not try to argue the validity of the approach her deceased husband would recommend but focuses instead on its utility (see Table 4.8) by suggesting the client might conduct a 'behavioural experiment', practise 'dancing' and look at the results. Part of the art of cognitive therapy is the flexible use of the questions in Table 4.8.

In reviewing the client's investment portfolio the therapist should be alert that activities are included that not only bring a sense of pleasure but also give a sense of achievement. When the portfolio is too narrow the therapist should explore a broader portfolio thus:

THERAPIST: It's great that you are enjoying visiting the ex-neighbour and reading some novels, what about expanding these activities to include things that might give you a sense of achievement?

SARAH: I should start to do something with the garden, that was always Mark's job and I can't bring myself to do it yet. But I could do some reading on advanced life saving, I was due to go on my 3-year renewal course around the time of Mark's death.

THERAPIST: That sounds a good idea and maybe just a little gardening, say weeding where you might place bulbs?

SARAH: I can give them a try. Do you still want me to use the MOOD chart?

THERAPIST: Oh yes, I am assuming you will automatically do the homework from previous sessions as well as new homework. They all build on each other. In using the MOOD chart, question your thoughts in the way I have questioned yours in the session by asking, how useful is that thought? Is it just me who would think this way in this situation, what would Mark say? (i.e. looking at the authority for what you say to yourself) and how true is this way of thinking?

Sixth interview

The sixth interview is outlined in Table 4.10.

Whilst the initial case formulation is a starting point for guiding therapy, as therapy progresses it is not uncommon to unearth other pertinent silent assumptions that also need to be a therapeutic target. Such assumptions can be discovered from an examination of the minutiae of the depressed client's inactivity or dips in mood. Thus the initial case formulation is simply a working model refined in the light of new data. This is illustrated in the following exchange:

THERAPIST: How did you get on with scheduling in activities to give you a sense of achievement?

SARAH: Oh, I did some weeding, it really needed doing, I was pleased about that.

THERAPIST: Good. What about reading about the advanced life saving?

SARAH (eyes filling): Couldn't bring myself to do it.

THERAPIST: What is it about that that is getting to you?

SARAH: I don't think I should be doing it.

THERAPIST: Why?

SARAH: My confidence is gone.

THERAPIST: Why?

SARAH: I think if I had attended more to Mark's headaches before his aneurysm he wouldn't have died.

THERAPIST: Has anyone else said that?

SARAH: No.

THERAPIST: Why haven't others said his aneurysm was foreseeable?

SARAH: Because they can just happen out of the blue.

THERAPIST: How often have you had headaches in the past and taken some paracetamol and been OK?

SARAH: Loads of times.

Table 4.10 Sixth interview

1. Same format as above
2. Targeting key silent assumptions
3. Tolerating the discomfort of acting opposite to the silent assumptions, managing rather than eliminating the dysfunctional core beliefs
4. Review use of MOOD
5. Further homework for depression and any co-morbid disorder

THERAPIST: How could you have known it was going to be any different with Mark just before he died?

SARAH: I couldn't but I feel so responsible so guilty, I've let Mark down and the children.

THERAPIST: Can you be truly guilty if you cannot foresee the consequences?

SARAH: No, but I feel it, it is tearing me apart.

THERAPIST: Does feeling guilty mean you are guilty?

SARAH: No. But I still feel it.

THERAPIST: Maybe the problem is not so much the guilt feeling but how you look at the guilt feeling, thoughts about thoughts or feelings, we call meta-cognitions and these can be faulty, e.g. 'I ought to take all my guilt feelings seriously'. What you can do is cross-examine these negative meta-cognitions in the way you did the first thoughts on the MOOD chart, come up with more objective meta-cognitions, e.g. feeling guilty doesn't necessarily mean I'm guilty', and then using the D of MOOD, decide what to do, e.g. just treat the guilt feelings as a mental cold, anticipating that they will take care of themselves.

SARAH: Some days I just brood on them.

THERAPIST: Well you could experiment with playing them differently.

SARAH: OK.

THERAPIST: For homework when you use MOOD also tackle any negative meta-cognitions but then make sure you change gear, the 'D' don't brood. Also continue to schedule in the activities.

An alternative way of challenging Sarah's guilt feelings could have been to see them as an example of her tendency to use the information processing bias of 'personalisation' (see Table 4.2), 'if something goes wrong it must be my fault', or again this could have been used to supplement the meta-cognitive focus. There is rarely just one way of challenging depressogenic thoughts.

Interviews 7 and 8

The seventh interview is outlined in Table 4.11.

The seventh and eighth sessions are similar to previous sessions in that they begin with a review of homework assignments; however, there is no pre-planned new teaching and the client's current concerns dominate the agenda. This should not mean, however, that these sessions lack focus. The therapist

Table 4.11 Seventh interview

1. Increasing delegation of responsibility for setting the agenda to the client
2. Increase responsibility for homework to client
3. Managing the silent assumptions/core beliefs

should be mindful that these concerns can be focused upon using not only cognitive therapy but also other members of the cognitive behaviour therapy family such as self-instruction training (Meichenbaum 1985), problem solving therapy (PST, Nezu *et al.* 1989) and schema-focused therapy (Young *et al.* 2001). PST involves teaching clients a model of problem solving that involves the following stages: problem orientation, problem definition, generation of alternatives, decision making, solution implementation and verification. In PST the client recycles to the menu of alternatives if the chosen solution has not worked or only partially worked and then tries another or a new alternative. Nezu (1986) and Nezu and Perri (1989) have published the results of two randomised controlled trials of PST for depression and found that it was superior to a waiting list and to an abbreviated form of PST that excluded problem orientation. In the following extract a PST framework is used:

SARAH: I still don't know what to do about work, I just want them to retire me but they won't, they are so ungrateful for the years I've put in.

THERAPIST: Are you spending a lot of time going over this?

SARAH: I try not to think about it but I just keep going over and over it.

THERAPIST: I am sure you are right to think about it because it has implications for the care of the kids and your finances.

SARAH: I do for a while and then block it, I've always had a habit of burying my head in the sand.

THERAPIST: We do know that people who are taught in therapy to lock onto problems, what we call problem orientation, recover from depression more than those who do a runner from problems. But obviously agonising about a problem all the time is just going to make you ill, so we get people to go through a special problem solving procedure once they have locked onto the problems. This problem solving therapy has been found to be very good for people who are depressed. I think the first step for you is getting you to stay with this problem of return to work, i.e. get you problem orientated, and then go through the other stages.

SARAH: You mean get the ostrich to pull her head out of the sand.

THERAPIST (laughing): You could put it like that I couldn't possibly say! I thought last time you were wanting to be back at work for the sense of achievement and financially but it's the care of the children that prevents you going back, is that right?

SARAH: That's right.

THERAPIST: After problem orientation the next step is problem definition, spelling out what exactly the problem is, nothing vague. At the moment the problem of your return to work is a bit 'fuzzy', because the problem isn't really that you can't return to work, it is really that you can only return for the hours that fit in with looking after the kids, is that right?

SARAH: Yes, when they are at normal school I could only work from 9.30 am to 2.30 pm.

THERAPIST: So what you have done now is that you have brought the problem into a sharper focus, defined it more. The next stage is to look at the alternatives and we could make a list of the alternatives.

SARAH: I could just ask them again if they would retire me.

THERAPIST: OK we could put that down as one option. What other options are there?

SARAH: I suppose I could write to them telling them I can only work the hours the children are at school.

THERAPIST: Fine we could put that down as a second option. What about copying the letter to your Union and to some Equal Opportunities person in the Health Authority, if there is one?

SARAH: I suppose I could.

THERAPIST: Well that is three options so far.

SARAH: I can't think of any others.

THERAPIST: The next step after getting the menu of options is to go through the advantage and disadvantage of each option. What about just asking to be retired again?

SARAH: It would be nice, but realistically I cannot see them changing their minds, they are a shower of *****.

THERAPIST: OK one of the good things about the problem solving procedure is that it keeps you on track getting things sorted, not going off on one.

SARAH: I used to do that all the time when Mark was alive, he did the sorting out.

THERAPIST: The problem solving procedure can help you take a leaf from his book.

SARAH: OK, there is probably not much point in asking them for the same again.

THERAPIST: What about the second option of writing to them asking for school hours?

SARAH: I could give it a try, but they are not interested.

THERAPIST: How do you know they are not interested?

SARAH: I just know.

THERAPIST: That sounds like Jumping to Conclusions (see Table 4.2) that you read about in Burns' book.

SARAH: I do slip into those biases without realising. I suppose I could write to them for school hours.

THERAPIST: What about the third option applying for school hours but getting the muscle of Union and Equal Opportunities behind you?

SARAH: That sounds good but what do I do if the children are off school sick?

THERAPIST: Well we can look at that as a second problem that we can problem solve. The important thing is not to mix up the problems like a tangled ball of wool, take one problem at a time, sort it as best you can and then tackle the next problem. Even though you know that in solving one problem another is being created. So let's stay with getting school hours and using the same framework you can tackle other problems later.

SARAH: OK, I will go with the last option and cross the other bridges when I come to them, see how it works out if I have not heard from them within 2 weeks I will give Human Resources a ring.

In the above extract the therapist has integrated PST with cognitive therapy strategies to focus on the client's pressing concerns. Further the homework has arisen from the client rather than the therapist. The therapist has also implicitly challenged the client's silent assumptions that she has to either agonise about concerns or block them. Further the therapist has underlined a role model, her deceased husband, to help the client construct herself as a 'problem solver'.

Closing interviews 9 and 10 (up to 20 depending on progress to date)

The final interviews are outlined in Table 4.12.

Cognitive therapy only gained acceptance when it was demonstrated that a very significant proportion of clients, 70% in the Rush *et al.* (1977) study, completely recovered from their depression, following a 12-week cognitive therapy programme. A change in diagnostic status is likely to remain the acid test for referrers and clients alike. At the penultimate session the therapist should check the client's current diagnostic status but also complement the findings with re-administration of the BDI and DAS. The following exchange took place after the therapist had checked diagnostic status using the depression questions in the Pocketbook, Appendix D:

THERAPIST: Just going through the questions I went through originally, I would not now say you were clinically depressed, though you still get a bit down and sleep is a bit of a problem.

SARAH: I do feel a lot better and the sleep isn't helped by the kids!

THERAPIST: Looking at the BDI you scored 14, which is quite an improvement from your original score of 28 and fits in with my diagnosis that you are now no longer clinically depressed.

SARAH: But am I going to stay this way after I finish therapy?

Table 4.12 Final interviews

1. Check current diagnostic status
2. Client's distillation of main learning points in therapy
3. Identification of relapse precipitants and rehearsal of coping strategies
4. Client authors their own survival manual, budgeting for slips but avoiding full-blown relapses using the manual. End of treatment completion of BDI and DAS

THERAPIST: I would like to look at relapse prevention by getting you to write your own survival manual, which you would use rather like a fire extinguisher at the first signs of a fire. Because it will be written in your words you will remember better how to use it and if you regularly run through the manual that will keep it familiar. As a guide to writing the survival manual, I would like to go through 'Recovered but . . .' (therapist hands Sarah a copy of Appendix I).

THERAPIST: Looking at the first item in 'Recovered but . . .' are there any situations in which you anticipate yourself slipping?

SARAH: I am sure I will get down at anniversaries and Christmas but I've just got to hear Mark pushing me to get on, but it will cut through me I just want to touch him one more time (tears).

THERAPIST: I am sure you are going to have your moments, but if you get on and 'do' out of respect for Mark I am sure you will come through.

SARAH: Others like my ex-neighbour are getting on, so I'm sure I can, I mustn't just go into my shell.

THERAPIST: So you could write down 'Anniversaries and Christmas' for triggers, item 1 on 'Recovered but . . .' and for warning signs, item 3, you could put 'drawing into my shell'.

SARAH: For the fourth item, what worked best I could put 'use the MOOD chart'.

THERAPIST: You might find it useful to look at the manual say once a week at a fixed time to serve as a reminder?

SARAH: I wonder whether I will do this, as after therapy I will want to think of myself as well now?

THERAPIST: If people have had one episode of depression there is a 50% chance of another, realistically it is probably safer to regard depression as rather like having diabetes, you are OK provided you do certain things.

SARAH: I'd like to think of myself as cured.

THERAPIST: Well realistically the truth is probably somewhere between cured and unwell.

SARAH: Sounds like once again I am using black and white thinking.

THERAPIST: Yes it might be useful to put something about the biases you use at your worst in item 2 of 'Recovered but . . .'.

SARAH: I could write 'stop being an extremist, don't see myself in a terrorist uniform'.

THERAPIST (laughing): Sometimes a picture does much more than words. I'd like to look in a bit more detail at what else might go under item 2, perhaps write down the silent assumptions on the DAS that you originally agreed with (Table 4.13) because when you are motoring on them, you are more likely to get depressed. A way of taking the 'sting' out of these attitudes is to question their validity, utility and authority using the grid. You could use the grid (Table 4.13) when therapy is finished to get yourself out of slips in mood.

Table 4.13 Sarah's cross-examination of dysfunctional attitudes grid

	How true is this?	How useful?	By what authority do I believe this?
Taking even a small risk is foolish because the loss is likely to be a disaster			
If a person asks for help, it is a sign of weakness			
If you cannot do something well, there is little point in doing it at all			
If I don't set the highest standards for myself, I am likely to end up a second-rate person			
I should be upset if I make a mistake			
If you don't have other people to lean on, you are bound to be sad			
I cannot reach important goals without slave driving myself			
I cannot be happy if I miss out on many of the good things in life			
Being isolated from others is bound to lead to unhappiness			

THERAPIST: I notice from your most recent DAS that you don't as strongly believe these ideas now, but when you get a bit low these ideas can fuel your low mood. I think after therapy, like anyone, your mood will dip from time to time and you could regard them as little fires, the danger for you is that you could slosh petrol on the fires by buying into these ideas. I was thinking that you might put this in the survival manual.

SARAH: Fine.

THERAPIST: What else might you put in the manual?

SARAH: I think the most important thing I have learnt is to keep active, just 'do' and let Mark get a word in edgeways, he didn't in life maybe he can in death!

THERAPIST: Fine, that could go under what worked best, item 4, on 'Recovered but ...'. The survival manual is just one resource and item 8 on 'Recovered but ...' is a reminder to have a wide range of resources and you might make a note there to use Burns' self-help book *Feeling Good*.

SARAH: Yes, I found his list of the ten thought processes was so useful.

The final session involves a review and refinement of the client's survival manual, thus:

THERAPIST: The manual looks pretty good, but it might be useful to include something about problem solving to stop you agonising.

SARAH: I get into agonising without realising it.

THERAPIST: Maybe writing something like, 'don't agonise, get sorted, take one problem at a time'.

SARAH: Sounds good.

THERAPIST: Then write down a problem solving procedure (Table 4.14).

SARAH: If I could keep to these steps I wouldn't get lost in my own mind.

THERAPIST: Great, add that to the manual.

SARAH: Might well have to use these steps if work refuse to accept the shortened hours I propose to work.

THERAPIST: That is the whole idea of the manual, to have a set of tools you can call upon in case of difficulties.

SARAH: What, in case of fire break this glass!

THERAPIST: Yes, to stop the fire becoming an inferno. You will also need to put into the manual survival strategies for use in the event of a return of the panic attacks.

The sessions finish with a discussion of procedures to be followed in the event of a full-blown relapse and an underlining of the importance of bearing in mind item 8 on 'Recovered but . . .'.

When the basics fail

Though cognitive therapy is a very effective treatment for depression it is important for the therapist to bear in mind that only about 70% of clients completely recover (see Rush *et al.* 1977). So a therapist (or for that matter their teacher) should not automatically assume that because their client has failed to recover it necessarily means they have been unskilful. The therapist has to guard against 'personalisation' (assuming that just because something has gone wrong it must be their fault, see Table 4.2) as much as the client.

Table 4.14 Steps in problem solving

What exactly is the problem? No fuzzies.
What are the options?
What are the advantages and disadvantages of each option?
What is the best or least worst option?
How could I put this option into practice?
Give the chosen option a chance to work and if necessary try a further option.

Table 4.15 Poor candidates for standard cognitive therapy (adapted from Young 1994)

1. An inability to report their feelings
2. Inability to report their automatic thoughts and/or denial of images
3. An absence of specific target problems
4. Lack of commitment to homework exercises and the learning of self-control strategies
5. Inability to speedily form a relationship with a therapist
6. Clients who reflect the dynamics of their poor relationship with others significantly in their relationship with the therapist
7. Clients who insist that their beliefs and behaviour patterns are part of the very fabric of their being and are therefore unchangeable

Young (1994) has suggested that poor candidates for standard cognitive therapy may have a number of the characteristics, summarised in Table 4.15.

Young (1994) has developed his schema-focused approach in an attempt to compensate for some of the perceived shortcomings of standard cognitive therapy. In conjunction with Beck (Young, Beck, and Weinberger, 2001) Young has developed a schema-focused, second phase of cognitive therapy to help prevent relapse. It is possible that such a schema-focused approach may also be of benefit to those who have not responded to standard cognitive therapy. However, there is a dearth of evidence as to whether schema-focused therapy is a useful adjunct to basic cognitive therapy or whether it reduces relapse. At present the jury is out on the added value of schema-focused therapy in depression.

Chapter 5

Panic disorder and agoraphobia

CBT is a very effective treatment for panic disorder, with over 75% of clients becoming panic free by the end of treatment (see Clark *et al.* 1999). According to DSM-IV-TR (American Psychiatric Association 2000: 436) about 10% of mental health consultations are for panic disorder and approximately one-third to one-half have agoraphobia.

The hallmark of panic disorder is recurrent unexpected panic attacks, which reach a peak within minutes. They may result in avoidance of the situations in which the attacks occurred resulting in agoraphobia. In clinical settings over 95% of those with agoraphobia meet diagnostic criteria for panic disorder (American Psychiatric Association 2000: 442), and those who do not are fearful of incapacitation or humiliation from limited symptom panic attacks. In the DSM-IV-TR (American Psychiatric Association 2000) at least 4 of a possible 13 symptoms, e.g. sweating, shaking, fear of losing control, are required for a diagnosis of panic disorder; clients with fewer than the 4 symptoms are described as having limited symptom panic attacks. The likelihood is that the panic disorder protocol would also be applicable to many clients with limited symptom panic attacks. Detailed enquiry about the symptoms of panic disorder and agoraphobia can be made using the Cognitive Behaviour Therapy Pocketbook, Appendix D.

The presence of panic attacks does not necessarily imply the person is suffering from panic disorder. Panic attacks may occur in other disorders, for example a person with a phobia about dogs may have an attack on encountering the feared animal, but such attacks are situationally bound rather than unexpected and the person would not therefore be diagnosed as having panic disorder. Similarly if panic attacks only occurred in situations in which the person thought they were under scrutiny by others a diagnosis of social phobia would be given rather than panic disorder.

Panic disorder and other disorders

The disorder most commonly associated with panic disorder is depression, with 38.5% of panic disorder and 42.4% of panic disorder with agoraphobia clients also suffering from depression, in a study by Zimmerman *et al.* (2008). The next most common disorders associated with panic disorder were social phobia and generalised anxiety disorder.

The pressing question for practitioners treating panic disorder clients is: does this co-morbidity make any difference to outcome? Whilst in general co-morbidity appears to make a difference to outcome, studies that have examined the issue with regard to panic disorder suggest it has little or no significance. However, closer examination of the panic disorder studies suggests that they have had too low power to detect the impact of co-morbid disorders. The panic disorder studies have been conducted at specialist anxiety disorder clinics which appear to attract clients with low levels of co-morbidity. For example, in a study by Kampman *et al.* (2008) only 6.8% of the panic disorder clients also had depression compared to approximately 40% in a non-specialist centre in the Zimmerman *et al.* (2008) study. Given that there were only 11 clients (total population 161) in the Kampman *et al.* (2008) who were suffering from depression it is not surprising that they were unable to detect an influence for co-morbidity. From a practitioner's point of view it is probably safest to treat not only the panic disorder but also the co-morbid disorder(s), particularly as Zimmerman and Mattia (2000) discovered, clients do want their co-morbid disorder(s) treated.

Clark's model of panic disorder

The original model of panic disorder was developed by Clark (1986), and he posited that catastrophic misinterpretations of bodily sensations play a pivotal role in the development of panic attacks, e.g. seeing breathlessness as a sign of an impending heart attack. Later Salkovskis *et al.* (1996) introduced the notion of safety behaviours to explain why it was that panic clients fail to learn, from their repeated experiences, that their panic attacks have no dire consequences. For example, a behaviour such as holding on to something during a panic attack may prevent disconfirmation that the panic attack has no catastrophic consequence because the individual may continue to think 'I was only safe because I held on to . . .'. In Figure 5.1 Clark's model and Salkovsis' refinement are summarised.

Going clockwise, Figure 5.1 shows that when internal (e.g. heart racing) or external (e.g. supermarket queue) stimuli are perceived by the individual as dangerous then apprehension or fear occurs, which is in turn reflected in a variety of bodily sensations (e.g. nausea, sweating). If these sensations are interpreted catastrophically (e.g. as a sign of imminent collapse) then the perception of threat is heightened, setting up a vicious circle. Further the vicious circle may be fuelled by a safety behaviour (e.g. going to the toilet until there is no supermarket queue) which prevents learning (e.g. that the queue posed no threat, that they would not in fact have collapsed) that

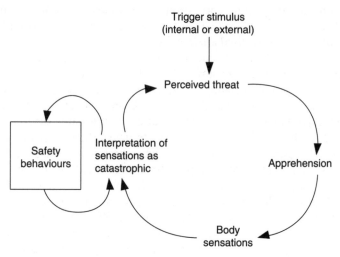

Figure 5.1 Cognitive model of panic disorder.

the catastrophic thoughts have no basis. Thus the safety behaviours ensure the recycling of catastrophic interpretations.

Some panic attacks occur without any obvious awareness, e.g. when a person might be asleep; thus the perception of threat and misinterpretation can according to Clark's model also occur at a non-conscious level. This is consistent with neurobiological models of panic which implicate the amygdala, the brain's alarm, which can process information at a non-conscious level, so that for example it is possible to feel threat but not know what the threat is about (see LeDoux 1998). Electrical stimulation of the amygdala can produce panic-like sensations.

A decade earlier Barlow and Cerny (1988) viewed panic attacks as 'false alarms' issued by the body in response to a cue or signal that the client has learnt to associate with danger or threat. Within both the Barlow and the Clark models the fear of anxiety, i.e. anxiety sensitivity, is seen as a vulnerability factor for panic disorder. The treatment approach of David Barlow and his colleagues has been to focus on increasing the tolerance of panic symptoms, by artificially inducing them – interoceptive exposure. It seems likely that both Barlow's and Clark's approaches work by reducing anxiety sensitivity but they do so in different ways. The treatment approach described in this chapter integrates both Clark's (1986) model and an updated version of Barlow's original protocol, termed Panic Control Treatment (Craske, Barlow and Meadows 2000).

Case formulation

To repeat a point made in the previous chapter a cognitive behavioural case formulation is a specific example of a cognitive model of a disorder. The first step in the case formulation is to determine what disorder or disorders the person is a 'case' of. The next steps are then to specify the precipitants for the disorder(s), identify the predisposing or vulnerability factors, determine the perpetuating factors and finally identify potential springboards or protective factors. In the previous chapter a case formulation was developed for Sarah but the focus there was on her depression; in this chapter the focus is on her panic disorder.

1. Diagnosis   To recap Sarah was referred 12 months after her husband died unexpectedly of a brain aneurysm. She was first screened using the 7 Minute Mental Health Screen, which suggested that both depression and panic disorder might be problems and were difficulties that she wanted help with. Following detailed enquiry about each of the symptoms that comprise the DSM-IV criteria set for the disorder, using the Cognitive Behaviour Therapy Pocketbook (Appendix D) and review of records, she was diagnosed as suffering from depression and panic disorder with mild agoraphobic avoidance. She was avoiding going to the city centre and going into crowded places; e.g. at her GP's surgery she would stand outside after having asked the receptionist to call her in when the appointment was due. Sarah began to experience unexpected panic attacks about 2 months after her husband died and they were ongoing at the time of the assessment with typically three a week. Initially Sarah scored 40 on the Beck Anxiety Inventory (Beck *et al.* 1993) a 21-item questionnaire that measures the severity of each symptom on a 0–3 scale; in particular she indicated that she was bothered a lot by the fear of losing control and of the worst happening. Her score was indicative of severe anxiety.

2. Precipitants   Sarah had not returned to nursing since her husband's death and was isolated in the care of her two pre-school children. The precipitating event for both the panic disorder and the depression was the death of her husband.

3. Vulnerability   Sarah had a belief that she had always to be 'strong' and that without this 'fight' she would not have survived her three miscarriages and stillbirth. Further she believed that being 'strong' was essential for her work as a nurse ('who wants a blubbering wreck, as a nurse?'). She therefore feared any experiences of fear, i.e. she had a high anxiety sensitivity, a vulnerability factor for panic disorder. In the previous chapter it was explained that she also had a vulnerability factor for depression that of an overvalued goal, 'normal, family life'.

4. Perpetuating factors   The diagnosis of panic disorder with agoraphobia highlighted the importance of Sarah completing the Agoraphobic Cognitions Questionnaire (Chambless *et al.* 1984) and she indicated that she usually thought 'I must have a brain tumour', 'I will not be able to control myself', 'I am going to pass out' and 'I am going to be paralysed by fear'. Though the depression pre-dated the panic disorder the latter was helping to perpetuate it.

5. Protective factors   Historically Sarah was a very resilient person, prepared to tolerate discomfort to achieve goals. This augured well for her learning to tolerate uncomfortable physical sensations of panic.

Panic disorder and agoraphobia Sat Nav

The panic disorder and agoraphobia Sat Nav in Table 5.1 is intended to help the therapist not stray too far from the effective treatment of the panic client and give direction when lost. Being at a loss in or before a therapy session is commonplace, albeit that it happens less often with experience, and it is useful to have a reference point at those moments. But as stressed in the last chapter, the Sat Nav is an aid and not meant to replace the session by session guidance given later.

Sarah first had a panic attack 2 months after her husband died. She was frustrated that there was no obvious trigger to the attack, she was at home looking out of her window at her garden when she suddenly felt hot, within a minute she became aware of her heart racing, felt as if she was going to faint and went and sat down. Though the attack lasted only a few minutes she felt agitated and confused afterwards, so much so that she went very early to collect her children from pre-school. However, at school she berated herself for inflicting such a long wait on herself. But Sarah was much relieved when she collected the children. On the way home she mused at how 'stupid' it was

Table 5.1 Panic disorder and agoraphobia Sat Nav

Therapeutic targets	Treatment strategies
1. Catastrophising about bodily symptoms	Normalising bodily symptoms
2. Anxiety sensitivity	Induction of panic symptoms
3. Avoidance of feared situations	Graded exposure to feared situations
4. 'Safety' procedures	Daring to gradually wean off 'safety' procedures
5. Intolerance of discomfort	Committing to goals, challenging 'catastrophic' cognitions
6. Dependence	Daring to gradually act independently
7. Relapse prevention	Personally constructed self-help 'manual', utilising key points from therapy and drawing on self-help books and computer assisted material

to feel 'safe' with her young children because if anything did happen realistically they would be an extra responsibility rather than an asset. That evening after she had put children to bed she had another panic attack. She pondered whether there might be something physically wrong with her and was mindful that her husband showed no obvious symptoms before he died.

Sarah booked an appointment to see her GP, who took her blood pressure; this was slightly elevated and suggested she had a stress reaction. Sarah was not however convinced as she had not felt particularly stressed at the time of the panic attacks. Sarah continued to have on average three panic attacks a week. She began avoiding crowded shops and the city centre as a precaution.

Using the Sat Nav (Table 5.1), the therapist's first task was to help Sarah normalise her symptoms. To this end the therapist recommended that she read Chapters 3 and 4 of Barlow and Craske's (2007) self-help book *Mastery of Your Anxiety and Panic* and planned to review with her what she had read at the next treatment session. In the sessions the therapist used a hyperventilation challenge, asking Sarah to stand, then breathe quickly and deeply to bring on many of her panic symptoms. Then the therapist posed the question that if she could bring on such symptoms could there really be something seriously wrong with her? Using the Sat Nav (Table 5.1), the therapist then addressed Sarah's propensity to live in the 'land of avoidance' rather than the 'land of approach' and gradually daring herself to inhabit the latter.

However, the therapist felt stuck in a therapy session when Sarah protested that she always had to make sure she had sufficient time to pick up her children from Nursery and therefore had to avoid going to the city centre. But glancing at the Sat Nav (Table 5.1), the therapist realised that this was possibly a subtle 'safety behaviour' and on further enquiry established that Sarah had no such misgivings prior to the onset of panic attacks.

Sarah completed a diary of her panic attacks and associated thoughts and found that during them she strongly believed that there was something seriously wrong with her brain but away from the situations she was much less sure. Whilst the therapist was happy that in the therapy session it was possible for Sarah to admit that it was unlikely that there was anything wrong with her brain, these considerations 'did not reach the parts that matter' at the time of the attacks. But looking at the Sat Nav (Table 5.1), the therapist decided that it might be worthwhile challenging her intolerance of discomfort by inducing panic attacks in the session and at the same time have Sarah import what she said to herself in her better moments. As a consequence of this she began to label her sensations as just 'sensations' and not as 'panic'. However, she felt that she could only do this in the therapy session as the therapist would 'stop anything really bad happening'. The Sat Nav, Table 5.1, then acted as a reminder to the therapist that Sarah needed to practise induction of the panic symptoms independently at home for her to develop a belief that she could cope with the attacks alone, i.e. this was the only way that ultimately her sense of self-efficacy could be enhanced.

The Sat Nav is however only a guide and there follows a more detailed session by session guidance.

Session by session programme

The procedures to be followed in the first interview have been described in Chapter 3; there now follows a session by session protocol for panic disorder with agoraphobia, from session 2 onwards. The programme draws on the work of Clark *et al.* (1999), Wells (1997), LeDoux (1998) and Craske *et al.* (2000).

Second interview

Table 5.2 outlines the second interview.

Sarah said she had felt understood at the first interview and was reassured that there were ways forward for both her depression and panic disorder. She said that she had also been encouraged by Chapter 4 of Barlow and Craske's (2007) book about panic attacks causing no physical harm. However, she still felt that there might be something seriously physically wrong with her, despite her GP's reassurances, and the following exchange took place in the second session:

SARAH: There could still be something physically wrong, couldn't there?
THERAPIST: How much of your thinking that way is due to Mark's sudden death?
SARAH: I'm sure it has a lot to do with it, but just because you are paranoid doesn't mean they are not after you!
THERAPIST (laughing): Hmm, it gets in the way thinking something is either in the body or the mind. You may have wound yourself up a little since the last session trying to convince yourself the panic attacks are all psychological, when you experience them in your body.
SARAH: I know, that's what I mean.
THERAPIST: We know that in all fear reactions, the brain's alarm, the

Table 5.2 Second interview

---

1. Inquiry regarding effect of first interview
2. Review of reactions to reading Chapters 3 and 4 of *Mastery of Your Anxiety and Panic*
3. Discussion of problems and accomplishments since previous interview
4. Description of neurobiology of false alarm
5. Using recent panic attack to illustrate the role of biology, catastrophic thinking and safety behaviours in the continuance of the attacks
6. Explanation of panic records
7. Inquiry to reactions to present interview
8. The setting of a written homework assignment including the tackling of any co-morbid disorder

---

amygdala, is involved. If you have had a lot of stress the alarm becomes oversensitive. It is as if the alarm becomes set in a war zone position rather than in a safe place. Your alarm/amygdala can then go off very easily. It can be tripped by external events such as being in a crowd or whenever there is any unusual sensation, e.g. breathlessness after running up stairs. The amygdala works both consciously and non-consciously, when you are awake and when you are asleep, so sometimes your sensitive alarm can be tripped and you won't have a clue what has caused it. But having a 'dodgy alarm' causes no physical damage.

SARAH: That makes more sense, I just knew my body was involved.

THERAPIST: The psychology comes in, in terms of what you say to yourself when you have these sensory experiences. They only become true panic when you catastrophically misinterpret them, put a 'danger, unexploded bomb' label on them. It is like being at a railway station and you notice an unattended bag and you are fine about it until someone suggests 'could be a terrorist bomb?'.

SARAH: Like when I tell myself I've got a brain tumour!

THERAPIST: I noticed on the Agoraphobic Cognitions Questionnaire that you often have that thought. Sitting here now how much do you believe you have got a brain tumour on a scale 0–100%, where 100% is total belief?

SARAH: About 40%.

THERAPIST: And when you're having a panic attack, how much do you believe it?

SARAH: About 80%.

THERAPIST: What would you think if one day you 40% believed someone had red hair and another day you 80% believed it?

SARAH: Something wrong with my eyes.

THERAPIST: The therapy for panic disorder is based on the idea that there is something wrong in how you focus your camera on your body sensations. What is happening is that you keep scanning your body for signs of any unusual bodily sensations, selective attention.

In this extract the therapist has conveyed the main elements of the psychology and biology of panic attacks and has also drawn attention to the role of selective attention in perpetuating the panic symptoms. The therapist then goes on to explain that agoraphobia is primarily an attempt to avoid situations in which the panic attacks may occur:

SARAH: I've had panic attacks nearly every day since the last session.

THERAPIST: Have they got in the way of you doing things?

SARAH: Yes, I really needed to go shopping on Saturday, I was out of bread, milk and potatoes but I waited until the Sunday because the supermarket would be less busy.

THERAPIST: Panic attacks do lead people to put 'danger' labels on all sorts of situations. So their life becomes restricted, this restriction is the agoraphobia. At present at least you are still going to the supermarket (even though you avoid busy days and queues) and the agoraphobia we would probably regard as mild. The more a person uses 'danger' labels the more agoraphobic a person becomes.

Whilst in the second session there is a necessary focus on the client's difficulties, it is crucial that their self-efficacy is bolstered, i.e. their belief in their ability to do things and make a worthwhile difference. Without an enhanced self-efficacy the client is unlikely to dare themselves to gradually approach situations they have been avoiding. Thus it is important that accomplishments such as reading the self-help material are praised and reviewed.

In the early stages of treatment clients are often vague about the frequency of their panic attacks. Their report of the attacks may be as much a reflection of a co-morbid depression as of the actual frequency of attacks. Further they may utilise the information processing biases that were discussed in the last chapter with regard to depression, overgeneralising about those panic attacks they do have. In the following exchange the therapist seeks a more detailed account of the attacks and to implicitly challenge a dichotomous view of them by introducing the panic record (Table 5.3).

THERAPIST: You were saying that you have had the panic attacks nearly every day since our last session, is that right?
SARAH: Yes.
THERAPIST: When was the last bad one?
SARAH: They were all bad.
THERAPIST: Was any worse than the others?
SARAH: Yes, when I was planning to go to the supermarket on Saturday morning.
THERAPIST: What was so bad about that?
SARAH: I thought I was going to faint.
THERAPIST: Did you?
SARAH: No, I just sat down.
THERAPIST: What I would like to do is a slow motion action replay of the worst panic attack and put the details down on the panic diary (Table 5.3). (*Blank record handed to Sarah reproduced in Appendix F.*)
SARAH: Looking at the diary the worst panic was on Saturday and that was about an 8, but I also had an attack the night before after I had put the children to bed.
THERAPIST: So if you were scoring the Friday night attack, on number 2 on the record, how bad was that?
SARAH: It wasn't quite as bad as the first, I would say a 7.
THERAPIST: You were saying that you had panic attacks nearly every day.

Table 5.3 Panic diary

I. Date	Time began	Time to reach worst

Physical symptoms...

What I thought?...

What I did? ....

How bad on a scale (0–10) where 10 would be the worst attack I have ever had?

....

2. Date	Time began	Time to reach worst

Physical symptoms...

What I thought?...

What I did?...

How bad on a scale (0–10) where 10 would be the worst attack I have ever had?

....

3. Date	Time began	Time to reach worst

Physical symptoms...

What I thought?...

What I did?...

How bad on a scale (0–10) where 10 would be the worst attack I have ever had?

....

SARAH: The only other one I can think of was staring out of the window looking at the state of the garden.

THERAPIST: OK we could put that down for number 3, how bad was that one?

SARAH: Probably a 6.

THERAPIST: So how long did it take for that panic attack to get to its worst?

SARAH: Oh I just felt I've just got too much to do and got more and more wound up as the day went on.

THERAPIST: A panic attack is something that reaches its worst within 10 minutes, it's a sudden rush of frightening feelings, it's different to the gradually escalating anxiety you began to experience after looking at your garden.

SARAH: OK.

THERAPIST: So it looks like in fact that you have had two panic attacks since the last session and some of your attacks are worse than others. One of the reasons we get people to complete a diary is to see just how frequent they are and how bad they are. As we go through therapy they gradually happen less often and when they do they are not as bad.

SARAH: I suppose I have been a bit dramatic about them, I just want them gone.

THERAPIST: I am sure we can get you back to a quality of life but it's likely that you will get a gradual reduction in the frequency and/or severity of the panic attacks, then a seeming back to square one, then more lasting reduction in panic attacks; progress does tend to be two steps forward and one back and you need to budget for this.

SARAH: So long as I can get there, I will have to take setbacks in my stride.

In the above extract the therapist is creating realistic expectations and inoculating the client against failure experiences. The diary (Table 5.3) helps the client identify the 'hot' cognitions that play a pivotal role in the development of the panic attacks and the compensatory safety behaviours that perpetuate the disorder. In the following dialogue the therapist takes the data from the diary about the worst panic attack to diagrammaticaly illustrate the panic cycle (Fig. 5.2).

THERAPIST: From the picture (Fig. 5.2) the catastrophic thought 'I am going to faint' led you to stay at home, but this safety behaviour stopped you learning that you would not have fainted if you had gone to the shops on Saturday. This then keeps going the idea that you will faint in the shop if you go on Saturday.

SARAH: I was planning to make sure I shopped on Friday.

THERAPIST: One of the main strategies in dealing with panic attacks is doing dares.

SARAH: Oh dear.

THERAPIST: I will just write down a number of things I would like you to have a go at both with regard to the panic disorder and the depression

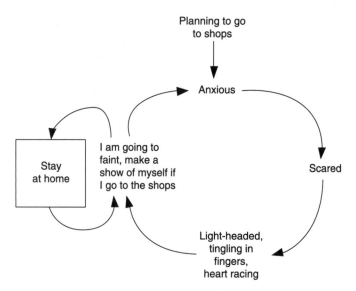

Figure 5.2 Example panic cycle.

'1. Complete diary of panic attacks; 2. Consider what you might dare yourself to do . . .' and review how you get on at the next session, is that OK?

SARAH: Fine but I don't know about dares.

THERAPIST: Only do little dares.

SARAH: I always avoided fairground rides! I suppose I could go to the super-market at a busy time on the Friday instead of an easy time.

THERAPIST: Fine.

In the foregoing extract the therapist checks out with the client the perceived viability of the homework assignment before concluding the session. If the client does not perceive that they may be capable of attempting the task, the homework will not be attempted, leading to demoralisation and a possible souring of the therapeutic alliance.

Third and fourth interviews

Table 5.4 outlines the third and fourth interviews.

These two sessions begin, like all CBT sessions beyond the first, with the negotiation of an agenda for the interview. Unless there are pressing reasons not to do so, e.g. the client is suicidal or has just been bereaved, the therapist is guided by the agenda in Table 5.4.

The panic diary (Table 5.3) can reveal the catastrophic cognitions, as can completed questionnaires such as the Agoraphobic Cognitions Questionnaire (Chambless *et al.* 1984). However, the catastrophic cognition may hide a deeper core belief and this needs targeting rather than its derivative. This is shown in the following extract from the third interview with Sarah:

THERAPIST: I noticed that on the Agoraphobic Cognitions Questionnaire you often think that you will be paralysed with fear.

SARAH: That is what puts me off going to the city centre.

THERAPIST: What would be so bad about being 'paralysed with fear' in the city centre?

SARAH: It would be awful.

THERAPIST: What would be so awful about it?

SARAH: I would be alone.

Table 5.4 Third and fourth interviews

1. Review of homework
2. Identification of catastrophic cognitions
3. Cross-examination of catastrophic cognitions
4. Behavioural experiments – hyperventilation challenge
5. Coping strategies
6. The setting of homework

THERAPIST: What would be so awful about being alone in the city centre?

SARAH: I would not cope if by myself in the city centre.

In the above extract the therapist has used the downward arrow technique, 'what would be so bad about . . .?' to identify the core difficulties. The key catastrophic cognitions can be cross-examined, in the same way as negative automatic thoughts, using the validity, utility, authority dimensions described in the previous chapter (Murphy 1984). In Table 5.5 a grid for cross-examining Sarah's identified key catastrophic cognitions is presented.

There is no hard and fast rule for using one question as opposed to another when challenging the catastrophic cognition, the skill lies in deftly moving from one dimension of questioning to another when it is unproductive. The strategies for Socratic questioning were described in the previous chapter, but are illustrated further with regard to panic disorder in the following extract:

THERAPIST: I have made a list of the ideas that seem to me to be fuelling your panic attacks (see Table 5.5); if you can imagine these ideas being injected into your head when you begin to have uncomfortable bodily sensations, what difference do you think they make?

SARAH: Like sloshing petrol on the fire?

THERAPIST: OK, there are a number of ways we can extinguish these 'inflammatory thoughts'; we can ask across the top (Table 5.5) either how true is the thought? Or how useful is the thought? Or is it just me who thinks this way? If we take one thought such as 'I am going to pass out', how credible is that?

SARAH: Well strictly I've never passed out. Just lowered myself to a chair to stop me doing so. But it feels like I am going to pass out.

THERAPIST: Have you ever fainted?

SARAH: Yes, in church as a teenager.

THERAPIST: What happened?

Table 5.5 Challenges to sample catastrophic cognitions

	How true or valid is this?	How useful is this way of thinking?	By what authority do I believe this to be so?
I have a brain tumour			
I will not be able to control myself			
I am going to pass out			
I would not cope if by myself in the city centre			

SARAH: Well I came over all warm, felt nausea and everything was slowed down. I went and sat at the back and someone got me a glass of water and I was OK by the end of the service.

THERAPIST: How like a panic attack was it?

SARAH: In a panic attack everything is not slowed down and when I fainted my heart didn't race and it wasn't a sudden frightened feeling.

THERAPIST: So the only thing in common between fainting and your panic attacks is that they are both uncomfortable.

SARAH: Yes they are very different.

THERAPIST: How possible would it be to tell yourself of the differences between panic attacks and fainting when you have an attack?

SARAH: Sitting here now I could say I would try but it could be very different when I am having an attack.

The above Socratic dialogue can sow the seeds of doubts about the validity of the catastrophic cognitions. Panic clients tend to not only see the consequences of having a panic attack in a given situation as catastrophic but to also overestimate the likelihood of panic in that situation. In order to counter the catastrophising the therapist can explain the physical significance of symptoms, e.g. telling the client that (with the exception of blood phobics) it is impossible to faint with their heart racing, as the latter signals an increase in blood pressure when a lowering of blood pressure is required for fainting. Clients can be asked to treat their predictions about the likelihood of a panic attack in a situation as a hypothesis to be tested out by encountering the feared situation. Further by being asked to record such exposure in the panic diary, together with the ratings for the severity of any panic attack, a message is conveyed that there is not a simple dichotomy of 'awful' panic attacks and being 'panic free', rather that panic attacks are on a spectrum many of which may be manageable.

Whilst discussion of thoughts that fuel panic is useful, the difficulty is that any modifications in thinking may affect only the background emotional state of anxious apprehension or fearfulness about the next attack and may not translate to the panic attack itself. During a panic attack there is a sense of imminent danger and this can be tackled by inducing attacks in the session and have the client test out their predictions. The following exchange highlights this.

THERAPIST: So you are not sure you could apply a new way of thinking in an actual attack?

SARAH: To be honest no.

THERAPIST: What I would like to do is see if we can bring on something similar to an attack in the session. So that you can test out your negative predictions. What I would like you to do is just breathe deeply and quickly for a minute and see what sensations you experience.

SARAH: *seated breathes deeply and quickly for a minute.*

THERAPIST: What do you notice?

SARAH: A bit breathless, a little light-headed.

THERAPIST: On a scale 0–10 how like a panic attack were those sensations, where 10 would be identical?

SARAH: Not much 3/10.

THERAPIST: OK let's try it again, a bit longer?

SARAH: *seated breathes deeply and quickly for 90 seconds.*

THERAPIST: How like a panic attack are the sensations you are feeling now?

SARAH: I feel more light-headed a bit nauseous, about 6/10.

THERAPIST: What do you think when you get like that?

SARAH: I'm going to faint.

THERAPIST: How long do you think it will take to faint?

SARAH: I don't know, I've never thought of it that way.

THERAPIST: Minutes or hours?

SARAH: A few minutes I guess.

THERAPIST: If we found that you did not faint in the next few minutes, what would that mean?

SARAH: My prediction is a fear not something based in reality.

THERAPIST: Let's focus on some other things for a few minutes and then come back to this.

SARAH: OK.

THERAPIST: The few minutes have passed, you do not seem to have fainted?

SARAH: No.

THERAPIST: For homework, I would like you to test out these negative predictions, when panics begin, ask yourself, what is the timescale on the catastrophe; for example, if you got the thought 'I am going to die' you would say 'by when?' and then if you thought within 2 minutes you could time it to see what happened.

SARAH: OK.

At the end of the third session the client is asked to read Chapter 7, 'Thinking skills', in Barlow and Craske's (2007) self-help book to consolidate the work done in the session. The fourth session is a review of the client's reading, how the client has been able to tackle the background emotion of anxious apprehension, the handling of panic attacks and exposure to feared situations. The following is an extract from the fourth session:

THERAPIST: I notice from the panic diary that you did go to town but had a panic attack in the coffee bar, which you rated a 6.

SARAH: I think I was very brave, going in on the bus I was telling myself, I don't know that I am going to have a panic attack there and so what if I was alone when I got there. It was mid-morning, so the town was quite empty, I was OK went into a coffee bar got to the till and found I only had a £20 note and the young cashier, couldn't have been more than 16, said she didn't have change because they had not long opened. I could feel myself getting all hot, couldn't catch my breath after searching through my bag for loose change I began to feel faint. Then the cashier said I'll go next door to the newsagents for change and off she went. I just wanted to die on the spot, I was all alone wondering what am I doing here, I felt faint but I remembered what you said 'by when?' and so I said to myself 'I will just stand here and see if I do faint by the time she comes back.'

THERAPIST: Great, so you avoided a safety behaviour like sitting down, to see if you really would faint?

SARAH: I was so relieved when she came back and pleased to learn that you don't faint if you just stand there. At its worst the panic was a 6/10 and I just sat down with my drink and thought why didn't I offer to pay with my credit card instead?

THERAPIST: I think that is what happens in panic attacks you put all of your attention on your bodily symptoms and miss what is actually happening outside of your body.

SARAH: Yes, after I sat down I just focused on the people going by, guessing where they were going, what they were doing and I was fine in minutes.

THERAPIST: In a panic attack it is useful to focus on something outside of yourself, such as a tree blowing in the breeze or a can of beans on a supermarket shelf, and just let the panic wash over you, like the tide coming in and going out, don't get into a battle with it, to do so is rather like revving a car stuck in mud. Use all your senses to describe what you are attending to, e.g. that can of beans is probably cold to touch, would make a noise if I knocked the cans into the aisle, if I opened the can it would smell of tomato and would feel very sticky if I put my hand in the can, might have beans on toast for lunch, need to get a nice cake to go with it.

In the above transcript the therapist has highlighted the role that selective attention plays in the development of panic attacks. Further the therapist has suggested an effective coping strategy, focusing on something external using all the senses in a spirit of detached mindfulness with regard to the panic symptoms. Some clients find benefit from diaphragmatic breathing during a panic attack. To achieve this the client puts one hand on their stomach so that their little finger is just above their belly button and the other hand is on their chest. The idea is that the client should practise breathing predominantly from their stomach, so it is mainly the lower hand that moves, counting on each inhalation and saying 'relax' on each exhalation. However, some clients feel that they may not be doing the exercise correctly and the strategy can be more of a hindrance than a help.

Sessions 5 and 6 finish with the setting of homework, involving the completion of the panic diary, daring to approach some feared situations and when doing so relinquishing safety behaviours, management of attacks using 'by when' and detached mindfulness, whilst the anxious apprehension is tackled by challenging the validity, utility and authority of the anxiogenic cognitions.

Fifth and sixth interviews

Table 5.6 outlines the fifth and sixth interviews.

At the fifth session the Beck Anxiety Inventory (Beck and Steer 1993) and Agoraphobic Cognitions Questionnaire (Chambless *et al.* 1984) are re-administered to check the client's progress and the client is given feedback thus:

THERAPIST: There's quite a reduction in the frequency of your panic symptoms on the Beck Anxiety Inventory; at the beginning it was 40 and now your score is 21, if we could get it into down further into single figures that would be great. On the Agoraphobic Cognitions Questionnaire you indicated that you no longer usually think that you have a brain tumour or feel you are going to pass out but you still usually think that you are going to lose control.

SARAH: I am getting better, I am more realistic but I still have a strong gut reaction that I am going to 'lose' it.

THERAPIST: Could you 'lose' it right now, go really crazy?

SARAH: What, roll over on the floor, scream?

THERAPIST: If that is what loosing it is, fine, just do it with style!

SARAH (laughing): I can't.

THERAPIST: Perhaps that is what you should say to yourself when you get this 'gut' reaction?

SARAH: Tell myself to really lose it properly, not just in a half-hearted way?

THERAPIST: Yes.

SARAH: I am not sure I would dare to tell myself that when I am by myself.

In the above extract the therapist has used paradox to help counter the client's persistent fear of losing control. Whilst some progress was made the

Table 5.6 Fifth and sixth interviews

1. Review of homework
2. Mid-therapy stocktaking
3. Ongoing cross-examination of catastrophic cognitions
4. Review of coping strategies
5. Facing physical symptoms: (a) inoculation; (b) practised induction – interoceptive exposure
6. The setting of homework

therapist has hit a roadblock, in that the therapist has become a 'safety' procedure and the client has a magical belief that the presence of a therapist or any person they trust will prevent dire consequences. This belief will also need tackling in the context of helping the client face their physical symptoms using interoceptive exposure. The therapist proceeds thus:

THERAPIST: What biologically is it about my presence or that of someone else you trust that stops the panic attack being extreme?
SARAH: I just feel more comfortable.
THERAPIST: How can another person stop the panic becoming extreme? Can they really be the equivalent of a paramedic armed with a defibrillator attending to a person who has had a heart attack?
SARAH: No I suppose not.

In the above transcript the therapist has had to challenge negative cognitions about having panic attacks when alone in order to facilitate interoceptive exercises that will disconfirm the catastrophic cognitions at a more experiential level. Thus the cognitive restructuring and behavioural experiments complement each other.

Barlow and Craske (2007) have developed a series of exercises that may induce panic symptoms. Clients are asked to perform each exercise for the given length of time and then to rate how similar the sensations experienced are to an actual panic attack on a scale of 0–10, where a 10 would be identical. The exercises and timescales are shown in Table 5.7; the exercises should not be attempted if there are any medical reasons not to do so, e.g. pregnancy, cardiac problems.

Those exercises that the client rates as producing sensations somewhat similar (a score of 5 or more) to an actual panic attack become the focus for helping the client face their frightened feelings. The rationale given is that trying to totally avoid frightening feelings has not worked; if it had the client would not be seeing the therapist. But that it is possible to become inoculated to the frightened feelings by inducing them on a regular basis rather like being given a travel injection that produces some of the symptoms of the disease but prevents the contracting of a disorder. The ill effects of the injection are tolerated for long-term gain. In the following extract the interoceptive exercises are negotiated for homework:

THERAPIST: You rated both the exercises involving movement of your head (the first two in Table 5.7) as 6's for their similarity to actual panic attacks.
SARAH: I reckon this is because in my worst moments I do get these stupid ideas about a brain tumour even though these bad times are not as often as they were.
THERAPIST: If you practised these particular exercises in the week it would

Table 5.7 Interoceptive exposure (adapted from Barlow and Craske 2007)

	Similarity to natural panic attack, 0–10
Shake head side to side (30 seconds)	
Place head between legs (30 seconds) and lift head	
Hold breath (30 seconds)	
Tense whole body (I minute)	
Breathe deeply and quickly (I minute)	
Run on spot (I minute)	
Spin in chair (I minute)	
Stare at bright light (I minute) then read	
Breathe through straw (2 minutes) squeezing nostrils closed by hand	

give you the opportunity to see the 'thoughts' of having a brain tumour as just that – 'thoughts' not facts.

SARAH: Practising tolerating the thought rather than getting in a state about it.

THERAPIST: Yes, your staring at a bright light then reading also produced a rating of 6.

SARAH: Again I suspect my not being able to focus – I maybe put that down to the tumour.

THERAPIST: You could add that to the list of exercises, together with breathing deeply and quickly which you also rated a 6.

SARAH: OK.

THERAPIST: When you do each exercise do it for just 30 seconds longer than you first feel uncomfortable. Then make a record of each exercise and record how bad each was on a scale 0–10. You could record them in the panic induction diary (Table 5.8), together with any thoughts you had at the time. The idea is that with repetition your scores will gradually come down. It is rather like being fearful of a dog as a child; the more often you go near it, the more the fear gradually goes down. Practise the exercises for 10 minutes a day.

The sixth session begins with a review of the interoceptive exposure homework. Failure to complete this assignment may reveal maladaptive panic attack cognitions, thus:

SARAH: I did the hyperventilation exercise each day and I am now much less bothered about the symptoms I get when I do this.

THERAPIST: Great, repeated practice really does lessen the fear. What about

Table 5.8 Panic induction diary

1. Date

Exercise practised

Time began   Time to reach worst

Physical symptoms...

What I thought?..

What I did?...

How bad on a scale (0–10) where 10 would be the worst attack I have ever had?

....

2. Date

Exercise practised

Time began   Time to reach worst

Physical symptoms...

What I thought?..

What I did?...

How bad on a scale (0–10) where 10 would be the worst attack I have ever had?

....

3. Date

Exercise practised

Time began   Time to reach worst

Physical symptoms...

What I thought?..

What I did?...

How bad on a scale (0–10) where 10 would be the worst attack I have ever had?

....

the other exercises, shaking your head from side to side and lifting your head up from between your knees?

SARAH: I didn't want to tempt fate.

THERAPIST: What would have happened if you had done the shaking of your head or head raising exercises at home?

SARAH: I've got to keep myself OK for the kids.

THERAPIST: So you didn't believe that you had the ability to do it and still be OK for the kids?

SARAH: I suppose so.

THERAPIST: So what exactly would you be unable to do for the kids if you produced actual panic symptoms?

SARAH: I just would not be very good.

THERAPIST: If they were ill would you still take them to hospital?

SARAH: Yes I would forget about me and just do it, it is too important.
THERAPIST: So if your attention is sufficiently on something you will just do it?
SARAH: Yes.

The above extract shows that the client's sense of self-efficacy can easily mar the practice of exposure exercises. In such instances the therapeutic task is to bolster the sense of self-efficacy and this can often be achieved by shifting the client's attentional fixation from themselves to something external. The panic induction diary can also reveal subtle safety behaviours such as having a drink of water or going to get fresh air after the induction. The homework task is then set again but minus the safety behaviours. The client's mood may also have become so low that they do not do the interoceptive exposure exercise, particularly if they have a co-morbid depression. Such dips in mood would need tackling using the strategies described in the last chapter, particularly using the MOOD thought record (see Table 4.4). To repeat a point made earlier, for clients with co-morbid disorders homework assignments will need to simultaneously address each disorder.

Seventh to twelfth interviews

The format for the last sessions is shown in Table 5.9.

The actual number of sessions required will depend on the extent of co-morbidity and on the degree of agoraphobic avoidance. If the client has a supportive relationship with a family member or friend, they should be encouraged to attend at least some part of some sessions and recruited as co-therapist. The co-therapist is in a position to encourage the client to engage with the homework assignments and ensure translation from therapy to the real world. For clients with more severe agoraphobic avoidance the co-therapist is particularly important, because they can ensure graded practice and encouragement in the client's natural environment. It is useful to explain to the co-therapist that their role is likened to that of a parent gently encouraging their offspring in a pool as they are learning to swim. Further that it is only by going to the 'pool' often that a real difference will be made. Once therapy is finished the co-therapist is more likely to be available to the client than the therapist and to be able to help ensure that slips do

Table 5.9 Seventh to twelfth interviews

1. Review of homework
2. Involvement of co-therapist, relapse prevention
3. Ongoing cross-examination of catastrophic cognitions
4. Review of coping strategies
5. The setting of homework
6. End of treatment assessment

not become full-blown relapses. In instances where a friend or family member is not physically available, telephone contact/e-mail with an informed supportive other can also constitute having a supportive other; this is illustrated below:

THERAPIST: Do you have anyone you can turn to about your panic attacks and depression?

SARAH: There's Marlene but she moved to Spain; she comes back about every 6 weeks to see her Mum who is ill.

THERAPIST: Could you share with her what we have being doing in the sessions?

SARAH: I could give her the written homework assignments to put her in the picture when I see her. I could even loan her the *Feeling Good* book because I know she gets down over her mother, feels guilty about living in Spain but there never was any pleasing her mother.

THERAPIST: OK, could you chat about the assignments and what you have read on the phone or by e-mail?

SARAH: Yes, it would be easy to do by e-mail.

THERAPIST: Would you visit Marlene sometime?

SARAH: I'd really like to but ...

THERAPIST: But what?

SARAH: I'd be afraid of having a panic attack on the plane.

At the tenth session Sarah's diagnostic status was checked using the Pocketbook (Appendix D) and she was panic free. Administration of the BAI revealed a normal score (less than 14) of 12 and the following dialogue took place:

THERAPIST: You have made great progress in overcoming panic, but I know you have concerns about the future such as having an attack on the plane and I would like to address these using 'Recovered but ...' *(Therapist hands Sarah Appendix I.)* This can help you construct a survival manual that you can refer to in the event of panic. I'd like to go through it with you and help you fill it in. You have already mentioned one of the possible triggers for a panic attack, going on a plane, and you could put this down on item 1, any other triggers?

SARAH: I am likely to get in a state on anniversaries and Christmas.

THERAPIST: OK put those down on item 1; item 2 looks at what you would likely start thinking to get in a panic, going back to your fear of getting on a plane what do you think you would be saying to yourself that would so frighten you?

SARAH: I guess it's the old chestnut, 'I'm going to lose control', so I make excuses not to go and see Marlene.

THERAPIST: On 'Recovered but ...' the third item refers to behaviours you engage in when beginning to slip, and it sounds as though avoiding making trips is an early warning sign you could put down.

SARAH: Yes, I need to watch these excuses.

THERAPIST: On 'Recovered but . . .' the fourth item refers to what you have found useful in the past that you could re-employ in the event of panic, what could you put there?

SARAH: The whole business of how likely is it that a panic attack will happen in a situation and even if it does it doesn't go anywhere.

THERAPIST: That would be great to put on 'Recovered but . . .', item 4; use 'Recovered but . . .' to write your survival manual and include all the homeworks I gave you and your MOOD records.

SARAH: Fine.

THERAPIST: Though you have mentioned how important it is to assess (a) the likelihood of a panic attack and (b) how truly catastrophic a panic attack would be, you don't really seem to have applied this to getting on a plane.

SARAH (laughing): Ahh!

THERAPIST: Have you ever had a panic attack on a plane?

SARAH: Not been on one since my husband died.

THERAPIST: So how likely is it that you would have one?

SARAH: I don't know, it's possible.

THERAPIST: If you had one, how bad would it be, on a scale 0–10?

SARAH: Probably only a 6–7, I'd just have to concentrate on the kids, maybe I'd be having to stop them fighting anyway in a 2-hour journey.

THERAPIST: Sounds a good way of coping focusing outside of yourself, but what is it that makes you think you could have an attack on a plane?

SARAH: I think it is the sense of being trapped.

THERAPIST: In telling yourself you could focus on the children you are really saying you are not trapped, you can take your mind off anywhere, the kids, a puzzle, a book, magazine, music, and just let the panic pass of its own accord.

SARAH: The detached mindfulness we have talked about.

THERAPIST: Another way of appreciating detached mindfulness is to think of the worry, e.g. suffocating on the plane, as being rather like one of your children being obnoxious when a worried visitor comes to your home, you have to concentrate wholly on their concerns, but you are very aware that there will be a time of reckoning with your child at an appropriate time when the visitor has left. Even whilst you talk to the visitor thoughts of your child might intrude but you keep your attention on the visitor.

SARAH: The children being obnoxious is very familiar!

THERAPIST: Are there any other situations you are avoiding that you did not avoid before the panic attacks?

SARAH: No, I just need to book a long weekend in the summer with Marlene and go for it, a new beginning, new start.

Chapter 6

Post-traumatic stress disorder

Over half the adult population (61% of men and 51% of women) experience at least one traumatic event in their lifetime, with 10% of men and 6% of women reporting four or more types of trauma (Kessler *et al.* 1995). Despite trauma being commonplace, only a small proportion, 10% of women and 5% of men, go on to develop post-traumatic stress disorder (PTSD) (Kessler *et al.* 1995). These findings are an apt reminder of the dictum of the Stoic philosoher, Epictetus, who in the first century AD said, 'People are disturbed not so much by events as by the way in which they view them'. This is not to deny that biological factors may also play a part in the variability of response to stress; indeed the American Psychiatric Association's DSM-V work group is considering classifying PTSD as a 'stress-induced fear circuitry disorder'.

Whilst PTSD is just one of a wide range of disorders that may be triggered by a trauma, it is unique in having a gateway stressor criterion (DSM-IV-TR, American Psychiatric Association 2000: 467). The stressor criterion requires that 'the person experienced, witnessed or was confronted with an event or events that involved actual or threatened death or serious injuries, or a threat to the physical integrity of self or others' and that 'the person's response involved intense fear, helplessness or horror'. The characteristic symptoms of PTSD, nightmares/preoccupation with the trauma, avoidance of reminders, constantly on guard, numbness/detachment are highlighted in the PTSD section of the 7 Minute Mental Health Screen in Appendix C. But such symptoms are just that, a screen; it can be very misleading to conclude that because a person has experienced an extreme trauma, say a serious road traffic accident and has say occasional nightmares of the incident and is avoiding driving that they necessarily have PTSD. To determine whether a person has PTSD detailed enquiry has to be made about each of the symptoms that comprise the diagnostic set; for this purpose the questions in the PTSD section of the Pocketbook, Appendix D, should be used. Without using such structured interviewing half of cases of PTSD are missed in routine practice (Zimmerman and Mattia 1999). The longer it is between a trauma and an assessment the more likely it is that the focus will be on the dramatic features that may have emerged such as alcohol abuse or psychosis or on aspects that the client feels are less painful to relate such as depression and which are more apparent to the therapist. Whilst these disorders may indeed be present, the PTSD and its possible pivotal role in the genesis and maintenance of the client's difficulties may be missed. Treatment strategies for clients with sub-syndromal levels of PTSD and for clients with PTSD symptoms but without meeting the stressor criterion, what Scott and Stradling (1994) have termed 'prolonged duress stress disorder (PDSD)', are described in Scott and Stradling (2006).

Nearly three-quarters of those with PTSD (70.2%) suffer from at least one other disorder (Zimmerman *et al.* 2008). The commonest associated disorders are depression (55.7%), social phobia (35.2%), panic disorder (23.8%), specific phobia (18.2%), generalised anxiety disorder (12.5%), substance/alcohol disorder (11.3%) and obsessive compulsive disorder (8.0%) (Zimmerman *et al.* 2008).

Cognitive behaviour therapy is an effective treatment for PTSD, with 70% of clients no longer meeting diagnostic criteria at the end of treatment compared to 16% of clients completing a waiting list (Bradley *et al.* 2005). Further follow-up assessments at 3 to 12 months indicate maintenance of gains. However, Bradley *et al.* (2005) also express concern that their review of studies showed that the majority of treated clients continued to have substantial residual symptoms post-treatment and they had doubts about the generalisability of findings because of restrictions on co-morbidity in the studies conducted.

Conceptualising PTSD

PTSD can be explained at different levels, the biological and the psycho-logical, but the explanations have to be consistant with each other. Further a model is of doubtful utility if it cannot be presented in a form that is readily understood by clients. To this end an integrated cognitive behavioural model has been developed by Scott and Stradling (2006) and has been made available to the general public in a self-help book, *Moving On After Trauma: A Guide for Survivors, Family and Friends* (Scott 2008).

There are two key anatomical sites with regard to PTSD: the amygdala and the hippocampus; together they form a threat evaluation system:

1   The amygdala, the brain's alarm, plays a major role in the fear response. Functional magnetic resonance imaging (fMRI) and positron emission tomography (PET) scanning have consistently shown that exposure to trauma-related stimuli provokes greater activation of the amygdala. The amygdala is also a seat of emotional memory and works on a perceptual matching rather than in terms of logic (LeDoux 1998). Thus a victim of a serious road traffic accident with PTSD might react strongly to the sound of screeching brakes outside his home, even though he 'knows' he is safe inside his home.

2   The hippocampus is responsible for putting events into context and draws on a store of long-term memories. Thus a PTSD client might remind themselves of their general knowledge that being in the house poses no threat.

Following trauma the danger is that the amygdala hijacks the threat evaluation system and the hippocampus is not able to inhibit the amygdala's overreaction, with a consequent ongoing sense of vulnerability and threat. Thus PTSD may be seen as involving a maladaptive functioning of the threat evaluation system.

Brewin *et al.* (1996) have distinguished two types of memory: verbally accessible memories (VAMs) and situationally accessible memories (SAMs); the first uses language and the second is a sensory memory. It thus appears that the currency of the amygdala is SAMs and that of the hippocampus, VAMs. In a cognitive behaviour therapy interview, the therapist is using language to help the client reconsider their VAMs; for example, the therapist might suggest that though the client was in an awful accident they did in fact make a difference by avoiding hitting a second car. As such the cognitive restructuring involves an empowering of the VAMs so that it is better able to regulate the SAMs. In a complementary fashion the 'grip' of the amygdala might be loosened by creating alternative and competing associations of the stimuli, e.g. by driving on a motorway and learning experientially that very serious accidents do not usually happen there. Successful CBT programmes for PTSD have involved exposure therapy, cognitive restructuring or a combination of the two, with no clear evidence that either form is superior to the other. It seems that the different forms of CBT operate on different anatomical targets, exposure therapy on the amygdala, modifying SAMs, and cognitive restructuring on the hippocampus, modifying VAMs. The programme to be described in this chapter has a dual focus on modifying VAMs and SAMs.

However, it is not only the threat evaluation system that is pertinent to PTSD; there is also a control-demand system consisting of the anterior cingulate and the dorsolateral prefrontal cortex. The control-demand system can in principle override the threat evaluation system to accept challenges despite fear. In this chapter therapists are encouraged to help clients take an adaptive meta-cognitive perspective on their fear so that it becomes a fear that they are not afraid of.

Case formulation

The details of a trauma can so grab a therapist's attention that without a structured interview it is easy to focus on a sub-set of symptoms and miss the bigger picture. Diagnosis is a first step in assembling all the information that comprises a case formulation. PTSD is unique in that the diagnosis contains an implicit working hypothesis as to how the symptoms have come about. But given that not everybody responds to the same extreme trauma by developing PTSD, factors that make an individual especially vulnerable and factors that serve to perpetuate the normal debility following trauma have to be considered. Finally the client's strengths and assets need to be highlighted and drawn upon to help them manage their symptoms.

1. Diagnosis   Dan was screened using the 7 Minute Mental Health Screen (Appendix C) followed by detailed enquiry using the Pocketbook (Appendix D) and was found to be suffering from PTSD and social phobia. The severity of Dan's PTSD was assessed using the PTSD Checklist (PCL, Weathers *et al.* 1993). The PCL asks clients how bothered they are (on a scale from 1 'Not at all' to 5 'Extremely') by each of the 17 DSM-IV symptoms of PTSD. In a study of road traffic victims and sexual assault survivors (Blanchard and Hickling 1997) a score of over 44 best predicted who had PTSD, whilst in the original study by Weathers *et al.* (1993) of combat veterans the best cut-off score was 50. The scale is available for personal use without charge from www.ncptsd.com. Dan scored 60, well above the cut-off for road traffic accident victims. He also completed the Posttraumatic Cognitions Inventory (PTCI, Foa *et al.* 1999), in which clients rate their degree of belief in maladaptive trauma-related cognitions, on a scale of 1–7. The PTCI has three subscales: negative cognitions about self, negative cognitions about world and self-blame; Dan endorsed the items shown in Table 6.1.

Dan also had concerns about his anxiety-related symptoms manifested in social situations, blushing, and stammering, and assessed using the Social Phobia Inventory (SPIN, Connor *et al.* 2000) and Social Cognitions Questionnaire (SCQ, Wells *et al.* 1993). His social phobia is addressed in the next chapter.

2. Precipitants   Dan's post-traumatic stress disorder arose following an incident in which he was driving on a motorway at dusk, on a winter evening. It had just started to rain when he encountered a hold-up; as he braked he glanced at the lorry behind him and saw the driver leaning to his side,

Table 6.1 Post-traumatic cognitions endorsed by Dan

1. The event happened because of the way I acted
2. I am a weak person
3. I can't deal with even the slightest upset
4. I used to be a happy person but now I am always miserable
5. I am inadequate
6. I will not be able to control my emotions and something terrible will happen
7. If I think about the event, I will not be able to handle it
8. Somebody else would have stopped the event from happening
9. My life has been destroyed by the trauma
10. You never know when something terrible will happen

presumably adjusting his radio/CD player. He knew a collision was inevitable, tried to take evasive action but was hit, and then clipped the rear offside of the car in front which had a child in a baby seat in the rear; his car spun, he feared another collision, and came to rest up an embankment. The child in the back of the car that he hit died.

3. Vulnerability Dan had had a difficult childhood, his parents were in constant conflict. He saw school as an escape, a safe place, and worked hard at his studies. In his early twenties Dan found it hard at work to manage social situations where there was not a specific agenda and saw a psychologist briefly for social anxiety. He had been free of any psychological symptoms for 25 years at the time of the accident.

4. Perpetuating factors Dan's guilt feelings over the death of the child served to perpetuate his symptoms; he believed somebody else would have produced a different outcome. At the inquest he saw the distraught parents of the child and was haunted by this memory. Dan's life was now devoted to trying to avoid thinking about the incident and to avoiding driving or travelling as a passenger in a car. However, the work of Wegner *et al.* (1987) has shown that trying not to think about something has the opposite effect and in Dan's case served to perpetuate his PTSD.

5. Protective factors Dan had a great deal of support from his wife, two adult children and brother. He believed he had done well to survive his unhappy childhood and was determined to overcome his present debility.

PTSD Sat Nav

The PTSD Sat Nav in Table 6.2 is intended as an aide-memoire, giving the therapist direction when lost, but it is not meant to replace the session by session guidance given later.

Since the accident Dan had an ongoing sense of vulnerability; when he was at home he wanted to be out and when he was out he wanted to be at home. The therapist pointed out that as 'the safe place' was always somewhere other than where he was, the sense of vulnerability was largely internal rather than external. At the first interview the therapist suggested to Dan that he had a 'dodgy alarm' and showed him page 26 of the self-help book *Moving On After Trauma* (Scott 2008), which depicts the diagram in Figure 6.1.

It was explained to Dan that prior to his accident it was as if his alarm was over to the left but as a consequence of the incident it was now, over to the right – the hypersensitive position. In this position he was on 'sentry duty, on the lookout for the enemy' thereby impairing his sleep/concentration, making him easily startled and irritated if anything was not as it should be. Dan was relieved that many of his symptoms had such a simple explanation and

Table 6.2 PTSD Sat Nav

Therapeutic targets	Treatment strategies
1. Taking seriously the sense of vulnerability/threat	Distinguishing 'real' from 'false' alarms, elaboration of similarities/differences in response to reminders
2. Self-blame	Accepting that responses are a normal response to an abnormal situation
3. Nightmares	Updating account of trauma and correcting the fantasy of an even worse outcome
4. Flashbacks	Detached mindfulness, writing an updated account of the trauma or constructing and listening to updated account on audiotape
5. Avoidance	Daring to gradually venture into the land of approach
6. Isolation	Building bridges with others, communication guidelines, anger control
7. Mood	Use of MOOD chart to manage mood
8. Relapse prevention	Personally constructed self-help 'manual', utilising key points from therapy and drawing on self-help books and computer assisted material

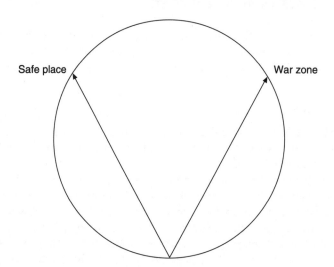

Figure 6.1 The brain's alarm, amygdala.

understood that the goal of therapy was to reset the alarm. To reinforce what was taught in the first session he was encouraged to read the first two chapters of the book for homework.

At the second session Dan's reading was reviewed and it was underlined that the amygdala is connected to a mini-computer in the top of the stomach, and that exposure to reminders of the trauma would trip the alarm probably resulting in a turning of the stomach or upwards surge. Further that since the accident his life had been devoted to not tripping the alarm by avoiding all reminders. But unfortunately the alarm could only be reset by gradually tripping it, feeling very uncomfortable at the time, but afterwards the alarm would as it were come back a 'notch' when it registered that no harm had actually come to him. In order to learn that external situations rarely posed a threat Dan was asked to gradually 'dare' himself to encounter the feared situations. This process was complemented by asking Dan to elaborate on the ways in which feared situations were similar and different to his accident.

Dan was encouraged to see his guilt feelings as trauma-related guilt rather than objective guilt and having a nuisance value rather than being a pertinent moral concern. This was reinforced by the therapist prescribing that Dan read pages 98–101 in *Moving On After Trauma*, to help him appreciate the normality of his response and to offer him a model of a client who was coping with such guilt feelings.

The therapist pointed out that dreams/nightmares are often about something that is not sorted out properly in the day and that in Dan's case his constant blocking of memories of the accident was preventing this 'sorting out'. Dan was, however, afraid that writing about the accident would 'swallow me up', so the therapist had him begin the writing in the session and it was agreed that at home he would write about it in his wife's presence. The therapist extended an invite for his wife to attend sessions whenever possible so that she would be better able to reinforce the within-session learning and compliance with homework assignments. However, Dan was concerned that his wife was getting fed up with him, particularly his isolating himself. The therapist then showed him page 28 in *Moving On After Trauma*, shown in Figure 6.2.

It was explained to Dan that he was bound to feel in a 'bubble' unable to connect with others if his body felt as if he was in a war zone whilst they felt they were in a safe place. He said that his wife Georgia was walking on 'egg shells', he could not be bothered doing things and if she encouraged him he would accuse her of 'nagging' and if left alone he would accuse her of no longer being interested in him. The therapist explained to his wife when she attended the third session that *Moving On After Trauma* is as much for the relatives and friends of the trauma victim as the victim themselves. At the fourth session the therapist asked Dan and his wife how they had got on with their reading and Georgia said that she found the rules for communicating very interesting as they were breaking every one! Whilst Dan acknowledged that the communication guidelines were important he felt the more pressing problem was to sort out his low mood, which led to inactivity and Georgia having occasional angry outbursts which lowered his mood further. The therapist explained that one of the consequences of PTSD is an alienation from others and an emotional numbness and pointed to the diagram on page 29 of

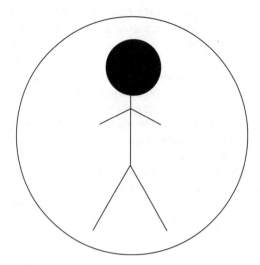

Figure 6.2 The bubble.

Figure 6.3 Emotional flatness.

Moving On After Trauma, depicted in Figure 6.3, of a half empty lemonade bottle.

The therapist explained that a major target in therapy was to get the 'fizz' back. In order to do this Dan would need to begin investing in life again but in small doses. However, even small doses of activity could be sabotaged by exaggeratedly negative reflex-like thoughts and in response to this Dan would need to develop more appropriate second thoughts. In this connection Dan was referred to Chapter 8, 'Managing mood' in *Moving On After Trauma* and the MOOD record (which has also been described in Chapter 4 of this volume). For both Dan and his wife *Moving On After Trauma* would be a workbook that they would become very familiar with in therapy and could therefore refer to in the event of slips post therapy to stop full-blown relapses.

Session by session programme

The procedures to be followed in the first interview have been described in Chapter 3 and they are integrated with the presentation of a treatment rationale for PTSD using Figures 6.1, 6.2 and 6.3. There now follows a session by session protocol for PTSD, from session 2 onwards; the programme integrates evidence-based exposure and cognitive restructuring protocols.

Second interview

Table 6.3 outlines the second interview.

Sufferers from PTSD spend a great deal of time trying not to think of their trauma and avoiding reminders of it. Consequently when they present for treatment they usually do so with very mixed feelings; on the one hand they want to get better but on the other they do not want to discuss the trauma. This can result in monosyllabic responses to the therapist's questions and the therapist may sense a certain hostility. In turn the therapist can easily feel 'stuck', knowing on the one hand that whichever CBT modality is used there is exposure but on the other that the evidence suggests this is necessary for the client's symptoms to resolve. Thus engaging PTSD clients tends to be trickier than in depression and the other anxiety disorders, as the following extract shows:

THERAPIST: Did you have any further thoughts after our last meeting?
DAN: Yes, it was OK. (As he said this he turned to look at his wife.)
WIFE (GEORGIA): Don't look at me, I wasn't here, he is asking you.

Table 6.3 Second interview

1. Enquiry regarding effect of first interview, review reading of *Moving On After Trauma*
2. Review of the 3 A's: Account of the trauma (including elaboration of worst moments), Avoidance and Alienation
3. Tackling Anger, the fourth A
4. Tackling co-morbid disorder
5. Enquiry of reactions to present interview
6. The setting of homework

DAN: (looking to the floor, silence)

THERAPIST: Did something get to you about it all?

DAN: It's made me think about it all more.

THERAPIST: What's so bad about that?

DAN: I can't stand that.

THERAPIST: So you are not sure that you really want to be here?

DAN: I guess so.

GEORGIA (with a deep sigh): good grief!

It is at such moments that the therapist has a strong desire for the alarm in the building to go off! The prime focus of the session then had to be on resolving the client's ambivalence to treatment. The therapist made a mental note to suspend items 2 and 3 in Table 6.3 until Dan could make some commitment to treatment. The session continued:

DAN: Of course I want to get better.

THERAPIST: But not at any price?

DAN: No.

THERAPIST: Overcoming PTSD is like having to exercise when you have a back problem; if you totally avoid exercising you don't get better but you could also make it worse by doing too much; what we do in therapy is let you control the dose of exposure/exercise.

DAN: That sounds better.

THERAPIST: The goal is to stop you agonising about the incident, because it is picking at it rather than thinking that is getting to you.

DAN: How do you do that?

THERAPIST: By looking at the incident and its effects as a 'sore', which needs to be sorted out and sharply focused on at a particular time as best you can.

DAN: Bit like a business meeting on something, rather than repeatedly dealing with an issue on the hoof.

THERAPIST: Yes.

DAN: Sounds OK, in theory.

THERAPIST: Because trying not to think about the trauma hasn't worked or you would not be sitting here now, we have to look at better ways of handling the memory and Chapter 6 of *Moving On After Trauma* has a chapter with just that title; I'd like you to read that chapter for next time, together with the chapter before it, 'Resetting the alarm'. I picked up from the start of this interview that relationships are strained and you might both find it useful to read Chapter 8 on 'Restoring relationships'.

GEORGIA: It's good to know it's not just us.

DAN: Yes.

THERAPIST: I mentioned at the first interview, Dan, that you were suffering from social phobia as well as from PTSD so you might also want to read the story of Karen in the book, who had both disorders and a problem-atic childhood, to get an idea of the pathways you can head along to get to where you want.

DAN: I will do that.

Thus though the session outline (e.g. in Table 6.3) gives a framework for the session, it should not be used inflexibly, and the emphasis should be placed on where it seems most appropriate.

Third interview

Table 6.4 outlines the third interview.

It is central to the cognitive behavioural account of PTSD that clients have incompletely processed the traumatic memory and a variety of means have been used to accelerate the information processing, from writing a page a day about the trauma and its effects (Resick and Schnicke 1993) to listening to an audiotape of the trauma until no longer distressed (habituation) (Foa and Rothbaum 1998), with no method superior to the other. For clients with literacy problems it has been found effective for them to dictate details of their trauma over four sessions and the therapist then hands them their 'biography' (Neuner *et al.* 2004). Another variation on these processing methods has been to have the client write a full account of the trauma once and read it aloud three times a day for homework (Maercker *et al.* 2006). Wells and Sembi (2004) have trained PTSD clients to note the intrusions but respond to them with a detached mindfulness, rather in the way that one might respond to a passing train, thereby allowing an automatic reflexive adaptive processing rather than blocking the memories. Following the second session, Dan, chose to write about his accident and this was reviewed in the third interview:

DAN: I kept putting off the writing, then when I wrote about I couldn't stop, had terrible nightmares that night. Couldn't face writing about it after that.

THERAPIST: I did say that if you were going to write about it, write for no

Table 6.4 Third interview

1. Review of previous session, homework
2. Review of the 4 A's
3. Engaging with traumatic material and feared situations without being overwhelmed. Review of remedial strategies
4. Re-authoring the account of the trauma and its effects – cognitive restructuring
5. 'Yes . . . buts', decatastrophising
6. Setting of homework for PTSD and co-morbid disorder

more than 20 minutes, no more than a page. If you go on longer, you can feel overwhelmed but you also lose a sharp focus.

DAN: How do you mean 'sharp focus'?

THERAPIST: Well you've written pages here, but if you had done no more than a page you would have been better able to stand back from your account and update it, but you get lost in details like how long you spent in the ambulance on arrival at hospital having to queue to get in, though that is bad it distracts from what seems to have really got to you which is what could have happened: 'I could have hit a second car, killed a second child, my children would be without a father'. What I want you to do with the traumatic memories is come up with an updated version, so that your mind accesses that rather than the old version that was recorded on the day of the incident.

DAN: Like replacing Windows 95 with Windows 2000.

THERAPIST: Yes, the old version is still there but when it comes on the 'screen' you switch to the new version; unfortunately it is not possible to delete a traumatic memory but we can teach you how to go around it and have a quality of life.

GEORGIA: Maybe I could help?

THERAPIST: Great maybe you could write for 10 minutes, Dan, discuss it with Georgia for 10 minutes then change gear, break off, say have a cup of tea or go for a walk?

DAN: That sounds better; I think when I did the writing it was too near bedtime. I'll do it earlier.

THERAPIST: That's good, there is a need to come up with a better account of the incident. Today I also wanted to look at your alienation from people and I suppose we have begun to look at that already to some extent by getting you to discuss the incident daily with Georgia.

GEORGIA: I found the chapter on restoring relationships in *Moving On After Trauma* very interesting and if we could keep to just one problem at a time when discussing a problem and stop mindreading I'm sure that would make a difference. But he won't answer the phone or go out.

DAN: I just blush or stammer.

THERAPIST: That is more to do with the social phobia than the PTSD and we can look at those things later in the session. Just to recap what we have looked at so far today, we have touched on the 3 A's: the account of the trauma, avoidance of thinking/writing about the incident and alienation. Looking in a bit more depth at avoidance are there any things that you might 'dare' yourself to do as first steps back to a normal life?

DAN: I couldn't possibly drive the car.

THERAPIST: Could you sit in the driving seat of the car on the driveway for as long as it takes to listen to a favourite piece of music, without moving off or maybe try a driving simulator at one of the big driving schools.

DAN: I suppose I could, but I can't see myself driving a car.

THERAPIST: Neither of us has a crystal ball, what about taking one step at a time and seeing what happens.

GEORGIA: He'll be unbearable like a bear with a sore head!

THERAPIST: That brings me to the fourth A I wanted to discuss, anger, the going over the top over small things. What I would like you to do Dan is use a 'Stop think relax' strategy, so that for example if Georgia suggests that it is time to do the writing about the incident before it is too late, as you are about to explode you shout STOP! to yourself, then 'THINK – is she really doing this deliberately to wind me up? Is it really the end of the world? And then RELAX; you can do this in whatever way you feel appropriate, e.g. sitting tensing and relaxing each muscle group in turn, putting favourite music on, imagining a very peaceful scene such as sitting in the shade of a tree on a summer's day feeling the light breeze and the grass.

DAN: So it is something on each of the 4 A's for homework.

THERAPIST: Yes but in addition I would like you to use a 'yes . . . but' when memories of the incident come to mind; for example, if you get an image of the distraught parents at the inquest you say something like 'Yes that was an awful sight . . . But no one there blamed me at all'.

DAN: OK.

Fourth interview

Table 6.5 outlines the fourth interview.

This session begins with a review of the client's progress in tackling the 4 A's the account of the trauma, avoidance, alienation and anger:

1 *Account.* Initially clients' accounts of their trauma are often overgeneral, reflecting a cognitive avoidance. For effective processing the account has to be graphic with the sensory details surrounding the worst part of the trauma made explicit. In such circumstances the therapist might explain that there is a need to move from a 'censored' version of the trauma to an 'uncensored' version and the writing of the latter would be set as a homework assignment. In the writing of the account many of the post-traumatic cognitions that serve to perpetuate the PTSD surface; a sample of such cognitions derived from the Posttraumatic Cognitions Inventory

Table 6.5 Fourth interview

1. Review of previous session, homework
2. Living in the land of approach
3. Immobilising saboteurs
4. Managing shifts in mood
5. Setting of homework for PTSD and co-morbid disorder

were presented in Table 6.1. Such dysfunctional cognitions are challenged using the Socratic dialogue described in Chapter 4; specifically the therapist can challenge their validity, utility and authority. Having the PTSD client write and then cross-examine their account of the trauma is an antidote to cognitive avoidance but clients also need to be encouraged to overcome their behavioural avoidance.

2   *Avoidance*. Clients' behavioural avoidance can take many forms from switching off the TV when there is a reminder of the trauma, avoiding the scene of the trauma, avoiding the context in which a trauma occurred to avoiding going out at all. The therapeutic strategy is to ensure that the client makes a commitment to living in the 'land of approach' rather than the 'land of avoidance'. They can be likened to two adjacent countries; initially the client is asked to just 'dare' to hop over the 'border' then gradually to dare themselves to venture further into the 'heart' of the 'land of approach'. It can be suggested that the client could choose to stay in the 'land of avoidance' for 'safety' but they are likely to become very bored, more depressed and isolated in that others have 'emigrated' to the 'land of approach'. It is thus possible to move judiciously between two levels of conducting cognitive behaviour therapy, that of challenging discrete cognitions (e.g. the post-traumatic cognitions in Table 6.1) using the framework of the MOOD record (Appendix E) and that of storytelling, changing the narrative.

3   *Alienation*. Although PTSD clients are concerned about their nightmares and flashbacks, in the long term they are often more concerned about the deterioration in relationships with those close to them. Further social support has been found to be the biggest single predictor of whether PTSD symptoms persist (Brewin *et al.* 2000). Encouraging clients to gradually invest more time in the company of those close to them is an important first step in bridging the gulf that has emerged between them and significant others. Unfortunately the home has often come to be associated with conflicts and the extra contact needs to be scheduled outside, e.g. going for a walk in the park.

4   *Anger*. Almost all clients with PTSD become uncharacteristically irritable overreacting to the most minor of hassles. If the client's anger problems are not addressed their alienation from others is likely to continue. The anger can be addressed at two levels: (a) background emotion – determining to what extent the angry frame of mind is a result of the frustration that arises from taking so many 'safety behaviours' or more metaphorically 'taking up residence in the land of avoidance,' and/or whether it is the result of a failure to organise their week in such a way as to get any sense of achievement; (b) coping strategies when encountering hassles. Thus the background emotion may be addressed by helping clients wean themselves off 'safety' behaviours and timetabling in of important tasks. Each task is broken down into small manageable

sub-tasks before beginning, with a celebration and ticking off of each sub-unit before progressing to the next task. In order to cope with minor hassles clients can be taught to 'STOP' and 'THINK' at the first signs of anger using an image of a tortoise which pops its head into its shell at the first signs of danger/anger. However, it is important to point out to clients that this strategy is an acquired art and they are very unlikely to be able to employ it perfectly, just sufficiently to maintain relationships.

At the end of this session homework is set that once again covers the 4 A's. Saboteurs to completion of the homework tend to revolve around self-efficacy, i.e. the client's belief in their ability to perform a particular task and whether the task would make a worthwhile difference. It is therefore important that the therapist bolsters the client's sense of self-efficacy by either pointing out similar past accomplishments or by treating clients' negative predictions simply as a hypothesis to be tested out rather than as representing a negative reality. Clients are also asked to complete and bring along the PCL (Weathers *et al.* 1993) and the Posttraumatic Cognitions Inventory (Foa *et al.* 1999).

Fifth interview

Table 6.6 outlines the fifth interview.

This session marks the mid-point in therapy and progress can be charted by inspection of the psychometric tests. By this stage probably most clients would be expected to be scoring below 50 on the PCL (Weathers *et al.* 1993) and symptoms that the client indicates still at least 'moderately' bother them (a score of 3 or more) can be targeted, as in the following extract:

THERAPIST: You have made great progress; your score is now 44 compared to 60 to begin with but I notice that you are still bothered by your sleep.

DAN: Yes it still takes me hours to get to sleep.

THERAPIST: It may be that you are not in the right frame of mind when you go to bed; try listening to music on headphones before you go. If you are not asleep within 30 minutes just get up and only go back when you are really tired so that bed is not associated with a battle.

Table 6.6 Fifth interview

1. Review of previous session, homework
2. Re-assessment
3. Review of MOOD records
4. Information processing biases
5. Connecting and communicating with others
6. Investing again
7. Setting of homework for PTSD and co-morbid disorder

In some instances clients are disturbed by dreams that are worse than what happened. Because such dreams are fanciful the client can be asked to vividly imagine the trauma in the early evening but integrate a fanciful ending, e.g. being greeted by a famous star after the incident. The message conveyed to the client is that imagining the worst case scenario is as bizarre as the positive outcome. Further the imagined positive outcome can also become integrated into the dreams, lessening the disturbance.

The post-traumatic cognitions can be challenged not only in terms of their content but also in terms of the way in which they manifest information processing biases (see Table 4.2) as follows:

THERAPIST: Dan, on the Posttraumatic Cognitions Inventory you indicated you still strongly believe 'You never know when something terrible will happen'; do you believe something terrible will happen in the next 5 minutes?

DAN: No.

THERAPIST (laughing): I am glad about that! But you did know that something bad would not happen in the next 5 minutes. I wonder whether you see things in extreme terms 'I am either totally safe or unsafe'.

DAN: What no in-betweens?

THERAPIST: Yes, it might be worth checking out this 'all or nothing thinking' when you are fearful. That is just one of ten ways of thinking that can help maintain your distress. For homework I would like you to read about them on page 99 of *Moving On After Trauma* and also read about the Communication Guidelines on page 87. You have stopped investing in things such as exercise and e-bay, buying and selling things; could you start these again?

DAN: I have got to; if I do not put something into life I will not get it out.

Sixth to eighth interviews

Table 6.7 outlines the sixth to eighth interviews.

These sessions begin as always with the setting of a negotiated agenda and usually begin with a review of the previous session and of homework. However, the therapist should be increasingly leaving the agenda up to the client and the latter given space to express concerns not already raised. A not uncommon issue for traumatic victims is that of pain and a client's perceived inability to manage this in turn affects their mood. Oftentimes a client

Table 6.7 Sixth to eighth interviews

1. Review of previous session and homework
2. Stepping around prejudice against self
3. Setting of homework for PTSD and co-morbid disorder

'blitzes' everything on 'good days' and is then unable to function at all for days; this abrupt alternation in activity levels results in total demoralisation. In Chapter 9 of *Moving On After Trauma* clients can read about how to pace themselves, how not to catastrophise about pain and how to influence the pain. A related issue is that because of the pain the client has not been able to perform sexually as they would have done before the trauma, often resulting in the cessation of sexual relations. This can be addressed by looking at the information processes biases in such a response, as in the following extract:

THERAPIST: So Dan you are saying you can't have sex now because you cannot kneel up, is that right?

DAN: Yes.

THERAPIST: Why have you got to have sex in exactly the way you did before?

DAN: I just have.

THERAPIST: Is this the 'all or nothing thinking' again?

DAN: I guess it is, I do it all the time with everything.

THERAPIST: I think that spotting that is very important, because in a sense it's not just about sex.

DAN: I feel so inadequate.

THERAPIST: I noticed on your questionnaire that you still strongly believe this.

DAN: I am inadequate in every way.

THERAPIST: But if you were not doing 'all or nothing thinking' about your sexual performance you might not be inadequate in that area?

DAN: I suppose not.

THERAPIST: Looking at the Biases on page 99 of *Moving On After Trauma*, I wonder whether you don't also tend to personalise matters: something has gone wrong, e.g. sex, so 'it must be my fault'.

DAN: I thought that when I was reading the Biases, I have being saying that because the child died it was my fault but there was no way I or anyone could have avoided hitting the car. But I still feel guilty but not as much.

THERAPIST: Maybe you have developed a prejudice against yourself and you have to teach yourself to step around this prejudice when it rises up, in this case by not taking guilt feelings seriously. For homework have a read of pages 101–104 in *Moving On After Trauma* which is about prejudice against yourself.

DAN: Fine.

Ninth to twelfth interviews

Table 6.8 outlines the ninth to twelfth interviews.

The final sessions address any outstanding issues but begin by recapping progress since the previous session and formal re-assessment using the structured questioning in the Pocketbook and re-administration of the

Table 6.8 Ninth to twelfth interviews

1. Review of previous session, homework
2. Re-assessment
3. Tackling outstanding issues
4. Distillation of protocol to be used in the event of relapse
5. Follow up interview, re-assessment, revision of skills

psychometric tests. The re-assessment ensures comprehensive coverage of all the PTSD symptoms and highlights where therapeutic attention may still need to focus, as in the following extract:

THERAPIST: (*from the Pocketbook*) Have you felt that you are not connecting with others, more than just a bit out of synch?

DAN: I am getting on much better with Georgia in every way, but I don't bother with friends and my brother the way I should. Stupidly, I get embarrassed but not as much now that I understand about social phobia.

THERAPIST: What could you do to bridge those gaps?

DAN: I could even call into my brother's for a coffee on the way home from here, me driving of course.

THERAPIST: Though you will drive you will not be a passenger?

DAN: I've got to be in control.

THERAPIST: (*from the Pocketbook*) Are you on guard a lot of the time, keep checking on things?

DAN: Yes, even when I am driving, keep checking in my rear mirror.

THERAPIST: What about for homework daring yourself to be a passenger going to your brother's, just focus on the licence plate in front and put on a favourite CD. Then when driving short journeys estimate beforehand how often you would have looked in the rear mirror prior to the accident and just look that often. The idea is to stop you thinking in the car so you are on automatic and not exhausted by the end of a journey.

DAN: I could give being a passenger a try, it is only 10 minutes from here to my brother's. When I am driving I could put a CD on as well and sing to it; that would stop me thinking too much.

THERAPIST: Great, they get soldiers to sing going into battle so they do not feel the fear.

In the above extract the formal re-assessment is woven into the fabric of ongoing treatment for outstanding issues.

'Inoculation' of the client against relapse is a major focus in the final sessions. Relapse can occur if the client encounters a reminder of the trauma that is seen as particularly salient. But relapse can also occur if there is a deterioration in mood. The reasons for the lowering in mood need not necessarily relate directly to the trauma, but entering the same emotional state that was present post-trauma results in directly accessing the traumatic memories. In general we remember material that matches our mood, a phenomenon called mood dependent recall. PTSD clients can become particularly demoralised by the return of flashbacks/nightmares if not prepared for them. To help focus relapse prevention efforts the therapist introduces the client to 'Recovered but . . .', Appendix I, thus:

THERAPIST: PTSD can be something of a ghost that haunts people; the incident has had such a big impact that you will never forget it but using the strategies we have gone through most of the time you will not re-experience it.

DAN: That sounds a bit ominous.

THERAPIST: Well sometimes the ghost returns with a vengeance in the guise of a particular reminder or as a spin-off of just very low mood. But with careful handling of the 'ghost' using this (*the therapist hands him 'Recovered but . . .', Appendix I*), it doesn't have the last word. I would like to go through it with you as the basis for you writing your own survival manual. The manual would contain the homework assignments and could make reference to pages of *Moving On After Trauma* that you have found particularly useful. You could reach for the manual when the 'ghost' returns.

DAN: To do a sort of exorcism!

THERAPIST (laughing): I hadn't quite thought of it that way. The first item refers to possible triggers; what do you think might trip flashbacks/ nightmares?

DAN: Certainly being in another bad accident but even seeing the aftermath might do it.

THERAPIST: Might do it?

DAN: Yes, if I am having a bad day a minor reminder might trigger the flashbacks.

THERAPIST: Going on to item 2, what would your thinking likely be?

DAN: If I was in another road traffic accident I would think it is a matter of time before I am killed and I would probably stop driving.

THERAPIST: So stopping driving would be an early warning sign and you could put that under item 3. What could you enter under item 4?

DAN: I would need to remind myself that I have dug myself out of a hole previously, I can do it again. I think if I felt shaky about driving again I might try one of those driving simulators first.

THERAPIST: What could you say to yourself to deal with the sense of threat.

DAN: I think 'if I behave as if I am in a war zone I will have no life, to live is to dare'.

THERAPIST: Sounds like 'Who dares wins'; on the 'Recovered but . . .' form there are also some reminders, items 5 to 8, that you might want to enlarge on in your survival manual.

DAN: Yes, looking at them it is hard not to want to think of yourself as cured.

It is useful to schedule a follow-up interview a month after the main treatment to ensure that the client is utilising the appropriate procedures to stop slips becoming full-blown relapses and to underline the utility of the relevant therapeutic tools and concepts.

Chapter 7

Social phobia

Social phobia is a common disorder with between 3% and 13% (DSM-IV-TR, American Psychiatric Association 2000) of the population suffering from it at some point. It is defined in DSM-IV-TR (American Psychiatric Association 2000) as:

> A marked and persistent fear of one or more social and performance situations in which the person is exposed to unfamiliar people or to possible scrutiny by others. The individual fears that he or she will act in a way (or show anxiety symptoms) that will be humiliating or embarrassing.

Clients can be screened for social phobia using the 7 Minute Mental Health Screen (Appendix C) and positive screens further examined using the social phobia questions in the Pocketbook (Appendix D). Whilst over a quarter (27.8%) of psychiatric outpatients meet diagnostic criteria for social phobia only 1.1% give it as the main reason for seeking treatment (Zimmerman *et al.* 2008). Social phobia is often co-morbid with other disorders; clients with the disorder have an average of 1.5 additional disorders, and over a third (35.2%) of those with PTSD suffer from the condition. Whilst social phobia is rarely the principal diagnosis clients do want such additional diagnoses treated (Zimmerman and Mattia 2000).

Cognitive behaviour therapy for social phobia has proven more effective than either the antidepressant fluoxetine and self-exposure to social situations or a pill placebo plus self-exposure (Clark *et al.* 2003). But for 30–40% of clients treatment does not work (Stein and Stein 2008).

The development and biology of social phobia

Behavioural inhibition in children, i.e. fear and withdrawal in situations that are novel and unfamiliar, has been found to predict the later development of social phobia (Hirshfeld-Becker *et al.* 2008), with 80% of sufferers developing the disorder by age 20. Social phobia is a risk factor for subsequent depression and substance abuse (Stein and Stein 2008).

In social phobia there appears to be hyperactivation of the amygdala and insula; the latter plays a central role in anticipation. Thus there are some similarities between the neurobiology of social phobia and PTSD; however only those with PTSD show hypoactivation in the dorsal and rostral anterior cingulate cortices and the ventromedial cortex-structures, which are linked to the experience and regulation of emotion (Etkin and Wager 2007), suggesting biological bases for the diagnostic distinction.

The Wells model of social phobia

The Wells model (1997) of social phobia proposes that when the social phobic anticipates or enters a social situation their negative automatic thoughts are of social 'meltdown'. The content of this 'meltdown' might involve variously, blushing, stammering, sweating, being incoherent or boring. The core of the model is the social phobic's perception of (a) what others remain focused on when they look at him/her and (b) the global negative inferences of others constructed on the basis of the social phobic's 'deficits'. Social phobics develop 'safety' behaviours to help them cope with these situations, e.g. avoiding eye contact, avoiding asking questions. But unfortunately for them such behaviours rarely work; e.g. others persist with communicating despite the avoidance, increasing the social phobic's sense of threat and accompanying distressing bodily symptoms, leading to a sense that 'meltdown' is imminent, often leading to escape. The social phobic's 'post mortem' on the social encounter often leads to a renewed commitment to avoid such situations. Because the feedback in most social situations is ambiguous it is difficult for the social phobic to collect information that contradicts how they see others seeing them. The key features of the Wells (1997) model are summarised in Figure 7.1.

Figure 7.1 indicates a number of points of entry for breaking the vicious circle of social anxiety, relinquishing safety behaviours, insisting that the client's perception of global negative evaluation by others should be evidence-based, challenging the client's view that others operate with a 'zoom' lens, making a global negative evaluation of them. Rapee and Heimberg (1997) have put forward a very similar model to that of Wells (1997); the core of their model is the social phobic's assumption that others have overly high expectations of them.

Case formulation

The details of Dan's difficulties in social encounters are summarised in the following case formulation:

1. *Diagnosis*   Dan's social phobia was first highlighted when the therapist conducted the 7 Minute Mental Health Screen (Appendix C) and confirmed

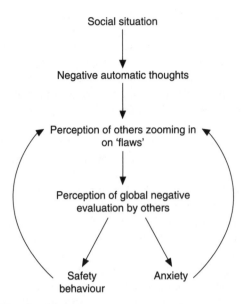

Figure 7.1 Model of social phobia.

by detailed enquiry using the Pocketbook (Appendix D); the latter indicated that social anxiety was not confined to one context such as eating in front of others but was a generalised social anxiety embracing all social domains. To gauge the severity of Dan's social phobia, he completed the Social Phobia Inventory (SPIN) (Connor *et al.* 2000). The SPIN consists of 17 questions which evaluate fear of: people in authority, parties and social events, being criticised, talking to strangers, doing things when people are watching, and being embarrassed; avoidance of: talking to strangers, speaking to people for fear of embarrassment, going to parties, being the centre of attention, making speeches, being criticised, speaking to authority figures; and physiological discomfort: blushing, sweating, palpitations, or shaking and trembling in front of other people. Each question is rated on a scale 0 to 4: not at all, a little bit, somewhat, very much and extremely. Dan scored 32, indicating a moderate social phobia (a score of over 19 is used to distinguish social phobics from those without the disorder). He was very bothered about blushing, sweating and shaking in front of others, particularly so in the presence of authority figures and strangers. Dan avoided being the centre of attention and he feared being criticised.

2. Precipitants   The trigger for his social phobia was a road traffic accident in which a child was killed.

3. Vulnerability   Dan had suffered from social anxiety in his early twenties and saw a psychologist briefly. His symptoms resolved within a few months following encouragement from his psychologist to socialise more with his colleagues at work. Dan had always found new social situations difficult and his social anxiety became more pronounced when he was promoted to an office job from working as a maintenance fitter. His parents had restricted any self-expression on his part and he had tried to hide away from the toxic atmosphere created by parental conflict.

4. Perpetuating factors   The diagnosis suggested that administering the Social Cognitions Questionnaire (SCQ, Wells *et al.* 1993) was appropriate. Dan indicated on the SCQ that he strongly believed: he was inadequate, he would babble or talk funny, he would be unable to speak, he would drop or spill things, he would tremble or shake uncontrollably and that people would stare at him. As a consequence of these beliefs he avoided social situations thereby failing to collect information that was contrary to them.

5. Protective factors   On a positive note Dan had previously overcome social anxiety and therefore most likely had the capacity to do so again, albeit that this might be made more difficult by his coexisting PTSD (the treatment of which was detailed in the previous chapter).

Social phobia Sat Nav

The Social phobia Sat Nav in Table 7.1 is intended to remind the therapist of the main therapeutic 'destinations' and the routes to be taken to these targets but it is not meant to replace the session by session guidance given later.

Since his car accident Dan had had vivid recall, not only of the incident but also of his 'total embarrassment' at age 20, at lunchtime on the first day of his new office-based job; he did not know whether to go off to the canteen with some colleagues or to go into the city centre by himself. He decided to go out and in so doing he bumped into his boss who jokingly said 'escaping from the mob', at which Dan stammered and blushed. He found it hard to eat as he thought of his boss thinking that he was an 'idiot'. On his return to work after the car accident this 'humiliating' incident from over twenty years ago had come back to haunt him, making him anxious again in social situations. Dan was cross with himself for letting such a distant memory have such an effect again.

At the first interview the therapist suggested to Dan that there are two very different stories of social encounters that people can use and depending on which one they tell themselves they will feel very different. The therapist drew Figure 7.2 to depict the social phobic's narrative (their theory of mind ToM).

Using Figure 7.2 the therapist explained that social phobics see themselves at the centre of everyone's attention, in Dan's case particularly that of authority figures. Further not only were they all focusing on him but they

Table 7.1 Social phobia Sat Nav

Therapeutic targets	Treatment strategies
1. Perception of what others think about them	Revisiting onset of belief that others negatively evaluate them and consequences, contrasted with utility of previous beliefs/assumptions
2. Information processing biases	Vigilance for all or nothing thinking, mindreading and inappropriate moral imperatives. Use of MOOD chart
3. Theory of mind (ToM)	Poor fit between client's official version of what is necessary to be acceptable to others with the actual behaviour of those they like. Rescripting ToM
4. 'Adolescent' self	Comforting, re-educating the 'adolescent' self that emerges in social situations. Coping self-statements – preparing for the stressor, encountering the stressor, coping with feeling overwhelmed, post-mortem
5. Social skills	Teaching client (a) how to keep a conversation going and to talk themselves using the headings 'general', 'specific', 'feeling', (b) the greater importance of non-verbal skills
6. Avoidance	Graded exposure to avoided situations
7. Relapse prevention	Personally constructed self-help 'manual', utilising key points from therapy and drawing on self-help books and computer assisted material

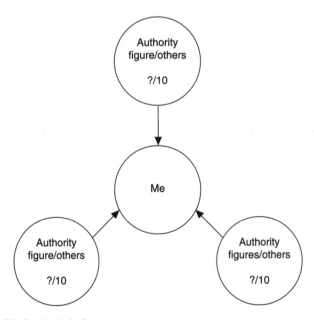

Figure 7.2 Social phobic's story.

were marking him out of 10 as a whole human being on the basis of his performance. The therapist suggested that if this was indeed the case it was enough to put anyone off social encounters. In this way the therapist sought to normalise Dan's responses. Figure 7.3 was then drawn depicting the story of social encounters that most people utilise most of the time.

Figure 7.3 illustrates that the main focus of others is on their daily concerns, e.g. whether they can afford a holiday, the last argument with their partner, etc. They do notice others in passing but rarely bother to mark them out of 10. Indeed most people can take or leave most other people most of the time; it generally takes too much effort to be for or against someone. It was explained to Dan that he had a choice as to whether he saw himself being scrutinised by others wielding a scorecard (Fig. 7.2) or the alternative theory of mind depicted in Figure 7.3.

At the second interview Dan revisited his first 'humiliation' and recognised that he had used the information processing bias of 'mindreading' (described on page 99 of *Moving On After Trauma* that he had been given to read after his first interview), in assuming that this boss had thought him an 'idiot'. However, such had been his social anxiety at work after the accident that he believed it was responsible for his being amongst the first to be made redundant.

In therapy Dan noted that his wife Georgia was very at ease in social situations, despite not having anything very interesting or witty to say. The therapist used this as data to challenge Dan's ToM that to be acceptable to

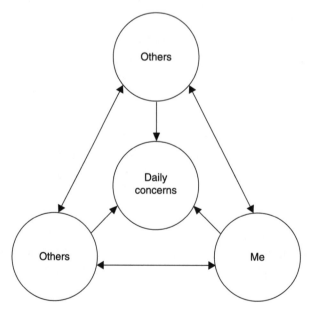

Figure 7.3 Usual story of social encounters.

others one had to be very interesting and witty, and suggested that this was an erroneous 'adolescent view'. Dan was encouraged to have a dialogue with the 20-year-old Dan to reassure him that he was unlikely to have been thought of as an 'idiot' given his subsequent promotions. The focus of therapy was then on rediscovering the social skills he had manifested after his first episode of social anxiety, followed by the practice of those skills in social situations he was currently avoiding. Finally Dan was encouraged to write his own manual for surviving social encounters and to use it as his reference in case of further difficulties.

Session by session programme

The following session by session protocol is based on Wells (1997) with material added on social skills training. The framework for the first interview was presented in Chapter 3 and the psychometric tests pertinent to social phobia were described above. Dan was asked to read the two case studies of social phobia in *Moving On After Trauma* (Scott 2008) at the end of the first interview.

Second interview

The protocol for the second interview is shown in Table 7.2.

With regard to Table 7.2 Dan said that though he had found it reassuring to read about two other sufferers from social phobia in *Moving On After Trauma*, he saw no point in confronting feared situations because he had done so at work after the accident with no success. However, the therapist was able clarify that Dan's goal state at that time had been to be as relaxed in social situations as before the accident. Because he had not achieved this by the time he was made redundant he regarded himself as not only a social failure but also as a failure in not being able to provide long term financially for his family. The therapist suggested that a more appropriate goal would have been 'mastery' rather than expecting 'perfection' in social situations – a 'good enough' rather than 'perfect' performance. Dan acknowledged that had he had the opportunity in work to practise at a 'good enough' level long enough he probably could have rediscovered his social skills. Thus the beginning

Table 7.2 Second interview

1. Homework review
2. Hierarchy of avoided situations, dares
3. Overestimation of danger
4. Catastrophising
5. Behavioural experiments
6. Revisiting 'humiliations'

of the second interview with Dan was devoted to preparing the way for him to conduct behavioural experiments with realistic yardsticks for judging success.

Dan and the therapist agreed that 'daring' himself to be around others in a work situation was his 'ultimate dare' and this was placed on the top rung of a ladder of dares. It was agreed that the bottom rung of the ladder might be to call in to see his brother on the way home from the session and the next rung would be for him to go to a café by himself. Therapy was described as a process of gradually climbing the ladder, sometimes needing to introduce intermediate steps if a step proved too difficult. In gauging the next steps the therapist was careful to clarify whether Dan was (a) overestimating the degree of danger and (b) whether he saw a perceived performance deficit as 'catastrophic'. If a client is making either of these mistakes they will probably not take the next step. Dan agreed to try both tasks for homework but was fearful that his memory of his 'humiliation' many years ago might overwhelm him. The therapist suggested he practise a detached mindfulness about it as opposed to blocking it, which produced a rebound effect (in the same way as he was advised to deal with intrusive images of his road traffic accident). Further the therapist suggested that he might be overestimating the likelihood of this 'humiliation' intruding in his brother's home and in a café and even if it did it was unlikely to be at a catastrophic level. The tasks are behavioural experiments to test out whether the imagined worse case scenarios really do unfold.

Third interview

The topics to be covered in the third interview are shown in Table 7.3.

The third session began with a review of Dan's homework. Though he had managed to visit his brother, when he went to the café he felt it was too crowded and did not go in. Using the metaphor of the ladder, the therapist suggested that perhaps this was too big a step and it might be more viable to introduce an intermediate rung by initially going to the café with his wife. Dan thought this was feasible and it was agreed as a homework assignment and the following exchange took place:

THERAPIST: What is it about going to the café with your wife that makes it easier?

DAN: Well I'll be able to talk to her instead of looking around.

Table 7.3 Third interview

1. Homework review
2. Climbing the ladder of dares
3. Identifying saboteurs
4. Use of MOOD for past and current social anxieties

THERAPIST: So how anxious you feel depends on where you put your attention?

DAN: I suppose so, I've never thought of it that way.

THERAPIST: Would others be looking at you any less because you are with your wife?

DAN: I guess not.

THERAPIST: So going to the café is really a way of testing out whether you can cope with others noticing you in passing and an exercise in focusing outside of yourself.

DAN: I just have to remember I am not at the centre.

In this session the therapist also introduces the MOOD framework (see Chapter 4, Table 4.4) for use in reviewing both past and current social anxieties and for homework. Dan was asked to read Chapter 8 of *Moving On After Trauma*, 'Managing your mood'.

Fourth interview

The structure for the fourth interview is shown in Table 7.4

The session began with a review of Dan's homework and he was pleased that he had gone to the café but was flustered when he ordered a latte and the assistant asked him which one, his mind went blank, he felt himself blush, there was what seemed to him an interminable silence before the assistant volunteered, 'small, regular, large' and he mumbled 'regular' in reply. He felt his hand was shaking as he began to drink his coffee. Dan said that he coped at the time by talking to his wife about how different their two children were with regard to mixing with people and how this might have come about. The therapist congratulated him on stepping up a rung on the ladder by going to the café and mastering the situation by keeping an external focus. Dan added that afterwards he struggled with his mood when he did a post-mortem about the café visit, and he then used the MOOD chart to sort himself out. He said that his first thoughts (observed thinking) were that he had 'made a show of myself by blushing and saying nothing', but he managed to have second thoughts (objective thinking): 'she has probably just thought I am thoughtful about which coffee to have and either not noticed my blushing or thought I was just hot'. Dan then decided not to 'pick' at his completed dare but to focus instead on doing something to lift his mood, enjoying the smell

Table 7.4 Fourth interview

1. Homework review
2. Mood monitoring
3. Behavioural experiments

of freshly cut grass as he mowed his lawn. For homework it was agreed that Dan would go to the café alone.

Fifth interview

The agenda for the fifth interview is shown in Table 7.5.

Social skills training is not included in all CBT programmes for social phobia, but the author has found it useful for boosting a client's sense of self-efficacy. When the therapist introduced Dan to the rudiments of social skills training he remembered that this was the treatment he had been given twenty years earlier but delivered in group format. He had found that it had given him the confidence to interact at work.

The therapist first introduced him to the prime importance of non-verbal skills and that in most social situations they are more important than what is said. By way of example the therapist said that exclaiming heartily 'yes!' at someone's good news was much more convincing than 'congratulations' said in a quiet monotone. Dan added that his wife Georgia was socially very skilful but never really said anything. The therapist suggested that in inter-action with others he could try to ensure an open posture, to communicate that he was open to what they had to say. Dan remembered that in his earlier group therapy they had talked about the importance of eye contact and realised he had reverted to avoiding eye contact with people at all cost. The therapist suggested he made eye contact 90% of the time when listening and 60% of the time when talking.

The therapist taught the following verbal skills: (a) repeating the last few words a person says and reflecting them back in order to keep a conversation going and (b) using phrases under the linked headings 'general', e.g. 'Are you going away?'/'I am going away', 'specific', e.g. 'where is that exactly?'/'up to Scotland', and 'feeling', e.g. 'do you like it there?'/'I really enjoy Edinburgh' to facilitate listening/talking respectively.

The therapist helped Dan put the non-verbal and verbal skills together using a role play of situations that he was likely to meet at an upcoming family wedding. In giving Dan feedback the therapist was concerned first of all to stress what he had done well and then to problem solve those parts that he was having difficulty with. Fortunately the role plays with Dan went very easily because they reminded him of his group therapy experience which had

Table 7.5 Fifth interview

1. Homework review
2. Social skills training: (a) non-verbal skills; (b) verbal skills
3. Role play/video feedback
4. Putting skills into practice

been a springboard to better social interactions at work. For Dan it was a matter of rediscovering lost skills rather than learning something new. (Alternatively Dan could have been videoed in role play and the results fed back to him as a correction to images of past humiliations that he was inclined to play in anticipation of and during social encounters.) He agreed to practise the social skills for homework at the family wedding.

Sixth to eighth interviews

The structure for the sixth to eighth interviews is shown in Table 7.6.

The sixth session for Dan began with a review of his homework assignments; he felt that he had coped surprisingly well at the evening celebration following the wedding albeit that he made an excuse to leave earlier than he would have done before his accident. He found that he used humour to deflect enquiries about how he was and remarked that this was the first time he had used humour since the accident. The therapist formally re-assessed Dan using the questions in the Pocketbook, Appendix D, and noted that whilst there had been a marked improvement in his social phobia in that he was much less threatened by conversation, he was still fearful signing cheques and indeed when he was asked to complete the psychometric tests in the session his hand noticeably shook and he blushed. These outstanding issues became the focus of the session. Dan was advised to drop his safety behaviour of increasing his grip on his pen when he felt he was under scrutiny because paradoxically this increased his shaking. Similarly he was so focused on not blushing in such situations that it produced exactly what he feared and so he was advised to deliberately try to blush as much as possible. For homework Dan was asked to complete the MOOD (Appendix E) chart in anticipation of having to write and to go to a supermarket and write a cheque.

Ninth to twelfth interviews

The number of further sessions needed depends on progress made to date and the extent of co-morbidity. The agenda for the final sessions is shown in Table 7.7; the final session is a follow-up conducted a month after the core programme.

The focus of the last sessions is on any outstanding issues. In Dan's case he

Table 7.6 Sixth to eighth interviews

1. Homework review
2. Re-assessment and re-administration of psychometric tests
3. Focus on outstanding issues
4. Putting it all together

Table 7.7 Ninth to twelfth interviews

1. Homework review
2. Client's distillation of main
   learning points
3. Writing of survival manual
4. Re-examination
5. Follow-up

was preoccupied with possibly meeting former work colleagues and was avoiding going to the local supermarket at busy times for fear of meeting them. It was agreed that Dan would begin testing out his belief that former colleagues had a low opinion of him by visiting a colleague/friend he had only seen once since losing his job.

Dan was anxious about therapy ending and the therapist invited him to construct a survival manual that he could refer to in the event of future desta-bilisation. The therapist introduced him to 'Recovered but . . .', Appendix I, to highlight the key domains that would need to be covered in a viable manual. Inspecting the first item on 'Recovered but . . .', Dan suggested that likely triggers for his social phobia were embarrassments such as dropping his change in a shop and he indicated on item 2 that his likely associated thoughts would be 'the assistant will think I am an idiot'. The therapist then asked:

THERAPIST: How would you know that social phobia has become an issue again? What would you enter under item 3?
DAN: I guess as soon as I avoid anything. But I do kid myself; I can see myself saying 'my wife can get the paper from the shop later', when in fact I am too embarrassed to go.
THERAPIST: Item 4 on 'Recovered but . . .' is about listing ways around the negative thoughts and avoidance behaviour; perhaps you can ask your wife to show you a yellow card if she thinks you are making excuses not to do something.
DAN (laughing): I think if I start that again it will not be a yellow card, I will be sent off the pitch.
THERAPIST: Under item 4 you could also make a written summary of what you had learnt in therapy.

For Dan his key learning point was that his reflex-like first thoughts about social situations were at best hypotheses and certainly were not facts. Dan resolved to construct his survival manual and mused that had he had such a personal manual following treatment for his first episode of social anxiety he might not have developed social phobia following the accident.

Chapter 8

Obsessive compulsive disorder

Whilst obsessive compulsive disorder (OCD) is rarer than the other disorders considered in this volume, affecting just 1.1% of the UK population (Torres *et al.* 2006), with 7.4% of those attending psychiatric outpatients suffering from the disorder (Zimmerman *et al.* 2008), OCD sufferers have more social and work-related impairments and make more suicidal acts (Torres *et al.* 2006). Sufferers from OCD alone are the exception (18.8%) rather than the rule, 81.2% having at least one additional disorder (Zimmerman *et al.* 2008). Interestingly in a comparison of OCD sufferers with and without depression, the two predictors of depression were level of functional impairment and the tendency to misinterpret innocuous intrusive thoughts as significant (Abramowitz *et al.* 2007).

Diagnosis

The recognition of a diagnosis of OCD tends to be very slow (Stobie *et al.* 1997). Routine use of the 7 Minute Mental Health Screen (Appendix C) can facilitate early identification of possible sufferers with confirmation of the diagnosis using the questions in the Pocketbook (Appendix D).

DSM-IV-TR (American Psychiatric Association 2000: 496) defines OCD as consisting of either obsessions (recurrent persistent thoughts, impulses or images that are regarded as intrusive and inappropriate and cause marked distress and which the person attempts to neutralise) or compulsions (repetitive behaviours, e.g. handwashing, checking) designed to prevent an event (e.g. contamination) or a dreaded event (e.g. burglary). To qualify for a diagnosis of OCD the obsessions must not simply be an excessive worry about a real-life problem and the compulsions must either not be logically connected with what they are trying to prevent or are excessive, e.g. checking that locked car door for 1–2 hours. It is possible to be diagnosed with OCD and suffer obsessions alone, with about 25% of sufferers falling into this sub-category (Freeston *et al.* 1997).

Monitoring change

The content of obsessions can vary considerably. The Yale-Brown Obsessive Compulsive Scale (Y-BOCS, Goodman *et al.* (1989), freely available for personal use on www.ocdrecoverycenters.com) provides a checklist of domains of (a) obsession: contamination, aggressive, sexual, religious, hoarding/saving, pathological doubt, need for symmetry or exactness and (b) compulsion: cleaning/washing, checking, repeating, hoarding/collecting, ordering/arranging, thus helping to target symptoms. The Y-BOCS has a 10-item scale that measures the severity of OCD symptoms and it is the most widely used outcome measure in OCD studies. A score of below 14 is regarded as normal (Anderson and Rees 2007); using the Reliable Change Index (Jacobson and Truax 1991), discussed in Chapter 2, a reduction of 10 or more points indicates improvement, a reduction of less than this indicates unchanged, and an increase of 10 or more points indicates deterioration. Only those whose score has reduced by more than 10 and who score less than 14 are regarded as recovered.

Effectiveness of CBT for OCD

Although the efficacy studies of CBT for OCD reviewed by Butler *et al.* (2006) suggest that 58–97% of sufferers improve, there is a serious problem in generalising from the results because some of the studies excluded clients with co-morbid disorders and some had no waiting list comparison condition. To circumvent these difficulties and determine the effectiveness of CBT for OCD, Anderson and Rees (2007) included clients with co-morbid disorders in a comparison of individual and group CBT with a waiting list. The group and individual therapy were equally effective and superior to the waiting list. However, using the criteria for reliable change discussed above and the Y-BOCS as a metric, 38.5% of those in CBT were unchanged, with 46.1% judged to have recovered and 15.4% to have improved; thus though CBT can make a real difference it is not a panacea.

A CBT model of OCD

The model of the maintenance OCD shown in Figure 8.1 is based on those of Wells (1997) and Whittal *et al.* (2002).

The obsessive compulsive cycle depicted in Figure 8.1 begins with a trigger. For example, a young mother with OCD might think 'I could throw the baby down the stairs'; this could have intruded into her consciousness for no obvious reason or as a result of an identifiable trigger, e.g. passing the top of the stairs. The CBT model of OCD postulates that individuals differ little in their intrusions but OCD sufferers negatively appraise the intrusion, e.g. 'thinking I could throw the baby down the stairs means I am likely to'.

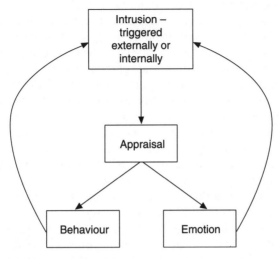

Figure 8.1 A CBT model of OCD.

Table 8.1 Obsessive compulsive cognitions

1. Inflated responsibility
2. Overimportance of thoughts
3. Excessive concern about the importance of controlling one's thoughts
4. Overestimation of threat
5. Intolerance of uncertainty
6. Perfectionism

Further the content of the obsessions tends to be in a domain opposite to that which the person values, e.g. a very loving young mum becoming preoccupied with thoughts of aggression. Aghast at the intrusion, the OCD sufferer might engage in a behaviour to block the intrusion, e.g. the young mum might think of a nice holiday, but after a very brief respite this serves to increase the frequency and intensity of the intrusion. The sufferer's distress at the intrusion also serves to generate greater access to the intrusion. Thus a vicious circle is set up.

The Obsessive Compulsive Cognitions Working Group (2005) has addressed the issue of the content of appraisals pertinent to OCD and identified the cognitive domains likely to be important in the development and maintenance of OCD (Table 8.1).

The above domains have been embodied in the Obsessive Beliefs Questionnaire (Obsessive Compulsive Cognitions Working Group 2005). In Table 8.1 inflated responsibility refers to excessive responsibility for safety or harm coming to others. However, Salkovskis (2008) has suggested that it is rather the sense of responsibility for collecting an overwhelming body of evidence that the feared outcome will not occur, i.e. the Elevated Evidence requirement, as opposed to utilising the more common gut reaction of 'it just feels right' in making a decision, that plays a pivotal role in the maintenance of OCD.

Wells (1997) has approached the issue of the role of dysfunctional assumptions in the maintenance of OCD from a somewhat different angle to the Working Group and Salkovskis, suggesting that for OCD sufferers it is not so much the content of their thoughts/images that is problematic but their evaluation of them, i.e. it is their meta-cognitions that should be targeted. Wells (1997) suggests that OCD sufferers are very self-conscious about their internal state, constantly monitoring it and setting inappropriate goal states, e.g. feeling absolutely certain. For example, the young mum may avoid carrying her child across the landing at the top of her stairs until she feels certain that she will not commit the dreadful act. As a consequence she may spend an inordinately long time with the baby upstairs. The meta-cognitive beliefs may take the form of thought–action fusions (TAFs). For example, believing that having the thought of throwing the baby down the stairs is as bad as actually doing it would be an example of a moral TAF, whilst believing that having the thought of throwing the baby down the stairs makes it more likely that the event will happen is an example of a probabilistic TAF. The TAFs serve to blur the boundaries between thought and action. Wells (1997) also describes a thought–object fusion (TOF), e.g. believing that thoughts of contamination can penetrate an object and make it harmful.

Case formulation

In Chapter 3, in order to illustrate the rudiments of case formulation, readers were introduced to Graham who suffered from OCD and depression; the evolution of his difficulties were summarised in Figure 3.1. In Graham's case the abuse he suffered as a child served as a vulnerability factor for both OCD and depression. OCD and depression have a different pattern of structural and functional brain abnormalities (Fineberg *et al.* 2007) suggesting a valid conceptual distinction between the disorders. Further OCD appears distinct from anxiety disorders in that the amygdala is not abnormally activated (Saxena 2003) in OCD. Thus in Graham's case it is important to draw upon specific CBT models of the disorders rather than employ a generic model.

Graham's OCD was triggered by being overwhelmed with work following his brother's motorcycle accident and perpetuated repetitive checking. He scored 25 on the Y-BOCS (Goodman *et al.* 1989) and also completed the Obsessive Beliefs Questionnaire (OBQ, Obsessive Compulsive Cognitions Working Group 2005). Graham's OBQ indicated an inflated sense of responsibility, excessive concern about controlling his thoughts, overestimation of threat, intolerance of uncertainty and perfectionism.

OCD Sat Nav

CBT treatments for OCD were initially primarily behavioural with a focus on exposure and response prevention in regard to rituals. Indeed in Graham's case the therapist taught him to use this strategy for his excessive cleaning when he came home from work. It was agreed that Graham could clean when he came home from work but only until the 7.0pm News. thereafter he had to tolerate the discomfort of things being 'not quite right'; this included not rearranging the magazines on his coffee table so that the edges were all exactly parallel to the edges of the table. Whilst exposure and response prevention is appropriate for overt rituals it is not feasible for covert rituals. When Graham volunteered that he felt compelled to trace his eye around the perimeter of objects and if interrupted had to repeat the procedure the therapist felt 'stuck' but looking at the OCD Sat Nav (Table 8.2) elected for a cognitive approach and enquired about what goal state Graham was trying to achieve by the 'tracing'. It emerged that Graham believed he had to have a sense of completion and he was encouraged to ask himself 'where is the evidence that I have to reach a sense of completion from tracing?'

Graham also had intrusive images of 'horror videos' of accidents occurring to his motorcycle customers and felt that he was therefore responsible for any accident (a moral TAF). Inspecting the Sat Nav, the therapist decided to construct a responsibility pie to disable this moral TAF. First Graham was asked what proportion of the pie should be assumed by the manufacturer for

Table 8.2 Obsessive compulsive disorder Sat Nav

Therapeutic targets	Treatment strategies
1. Model of mental life, thought–action fusion (TAF), attributing moral status to intrusions	Develop more appropriate model, decoupling fusion, emotional reasoning – the difference between feeling guilty and being guilty
2. Inappropriate goal state, e.g. absolute certainty, perfect cleanliness	Distilling achievable goals
3. Excessive responsibility	Responsibility pie
4. Bipolar functioning – perception of no choice (compulsion) alternating with perception of perfect freedom (leading to self-blame)	Encourage perception of reasonable degree of control by postponement strategies. Use of MOOD chart
5. Neutralising images, thoughts, behaviours	Exposure and response prevention. Behavioural experiments
6. Overestimation of danger	Distillation of realistic probabilities
7. Relapse prevention	Personally constructed self-help 'manual', utilising key points from therapy and drawing on self-help books and computer assisted material

any accident and he replied a third. Then Graham was asked what proportion of responsibility should the rider assume and he again replied a third. The therapist then put it to him that the most responsibility he could possibly assume for any accident was therefore a third. It was agreed that Graham would imagine the pie when he had intrusive images of an accident befalling a customer, rather than try and neutralise the latter image (which tended to intensify it). The therapist also targeted Graham's overestimation of danger by asking Graham how many motorcycle customers he had supplied; when Graham replied '1000s', he was then asked how many had come to grief because of him and he responded 'none'. This allowed the therapist to suggest that a more realistic estimate of danger was less than 1 in 1000 rather than using emotional reasoning (see Table 4.2, Information processing biases) to conclude that danger was imminent. The therapist also introduced Graham to another information processing bias, dichotomous thinking, which was creating his bipolar functioning – either engaging in a compulsive ritual or, if not, being debilitated by guilt. Graham was also taught to be aware of the information processing biases in tackling his co-morbid depression.

Session by session programme

The procedures to be followed in the first interview have been described in Chapter 3. There now follows a session by session protocol for OCD, from session 2 onwards. The programme is based on those described by Wells (1997) and Anderson and Rees (2007).

Second interview

Table 8.3 outlines the second interview.

The second session begins with a review of the model of mind, presented at the first interview. In Graham's case the second interview began thus:

THERAPIST: Did you have any thoughts about viewing the mind as like a railway station, you can't control what comes in, sometimes the train is late or makes a loud noise?

GRAHAM: I think I just jump down onto the track when I think of harm coming to others on a motorcycle I've sold.

Table 8.3 Second interview

1. Review of normalising intrusions
2. Countering belief that it is necessary and possible to control one's thoughts
3. Introduce concept of worry about intrusions rather than intrusions as the problem
4. Exposure and response prevention – discussion of tape
5. Homework including reading about an OCD sufferer in *Moving On After Trauma*

THERAPIST: So you just get mangled by the train.

GRAHAM: That's about it.

THERAPIST: What I would just like you to do is just let these trains of thought and images run their course.

GRAHAM: Easier said than done.

THERAPIST: What can be very useful is making a 2-minute tape of the thoughts and images and listening to it over and over until you are much less bothered by it.

GRAHAM: Sounds horrendous!

THERAPIST: It is not the easiest strategy and in all honesty about 50% of people are unable to tolerate it but if you can do it, it is very successful. We could try it first in the session, I could get you to dictate it into my dictaphone and we could replay it over and over. For today we could just record it.

GRAHAM: OK (*client dictates thoughts and images of harm and feelings of guilt*).

THERAPIST: The idea is that you teach yourself not to be afraid of these thoughts/images and can postpone them (without blocking) for consideration at the time you listen to your tape.

For homework Graham was asked to read about an OCD sufferer in *Moving On After Trauma* (Scott 2008) so that he felt less isolated and could read about a range of coping strategies for the OCD. In Graham's case the book had the added advantage in that it detailed strategies for coping with his co-morbid depression and its trauma focus meant that he could draw upon it in assisting his brother who had been debilitated by the motorcycle accident.

Third interview

The outline of the third interview is shown in Table 8.4.

At the second interview Graham reported that he had had some success in not repeatedly checking that he had left everything secure at home before leaving for work. It was agreed that he wean himself off this further by initially putting a strange label on the activity he repeated, for example

Table 8.4 Third interview

1. Review of homework
2. Exposure and response prevention in session
3. Reducing 'safety' behaviour as a behavioural experiment
4. Tackling inflated responsibility using responsibility pie
5. Tackling the emotional context for ritualistic behaviour using MOOD
6. Homework

saying to himself 'green igloo' when he had locked the door of his home, the recurrence of the phrase would remind him that there was no need to go back. Each ritualistic situation was to be given a one-off strange label, so that when he arrived at work and locked his car he said 'Arsenal-Rugby'; in this way he was able to avoid the hour or more that he could spend in and out of the car park. The therapist then proceeded to address in-session exposure and response prevention by playing the tape of Graham's thoughts/images and asking him how bad he felt on a scale 0–10 listening to it, i.e. he determined a Subjective Units of Distress (SUDS) score. Graham said he felt an 8 and the therapist asked that he listen to the tape over and over until his score came down by 50% to 4; in the event this took 45 minutes. The therapist then suggested he might make a loop tape of his thoughts/images (loop tapes are available from office supply stores and obviate the need to rewind the tape) and listen to it for an hour a day for homework.

Graham was discouraging visitors to his home for fear they would make his home dirty/untidy and the therapist focused on his dropping this 'safety' behaviour and testing out whether anything awful would happen as a consequence of their visits. It was agreed that for homework he would invite relatives over on Sunday afternoon for a barbecue. But Graham was fearful that he would become very apprehensive before they arrived and that he would therefore get into a frenzy of cleaning. The frequency of ritualistic behaviour is often mood dependent and so Graham was asked to complete the MOOD chart when he became highly anxious. Graham was also fearful of encountering his brother, who was not as Graham put it a 'happy bunny' since the accident. The therapist introduced the notion of a responsibility pie to help counter Graham's inflated sense of responsibility for his brother. After some discussion with Graham about his brother, the therapist asked:

THERAPIST: What proportion of your brother's difficulties are due to his drinking excessively since the accident?
GRAHAM: I think it is about half.
THERAPIST: What proportion to his wife.
GRAHAM: It's a difficult situation for her, but she could handle it better without the tirades, I think about 25%.
THERAPIST: That leaves at most 25% to be taken up by yourself or anybody else.
GRAHAM: Maybe I should have a quarter of a pie at the barbecue as a reminder.
THERAPIST: Having a regular reminder would be really useful.
GRAHAM: But I will feel bad having drink around with my brother being the way he is.
THERAPIST: It's a difficult one, but you might be using emotional reasoning concluding that because you feel guilty you must be guilty.

Fourth to sixth interviews

The format for the fourth to sixth interviews is shown in Table 8.5.

By the fifth session clients should be re-assessed. Graham scored 15 on the Y-BOCS (Goodman *et al.* 1989), indicating a clinically significant improvement in his condition but not quite scoring in the normal region. The therapist noted that in reviewing Graham's progress with the loop tape his initial SUDS scores were reducing, i.e. there was between session habituation and it was taking him gradually less time to reduce his SUDS by 50%.

In these interviews Graham was introduced to the concept of detached mindfulness, i.e. to become aware of intrusions without getting hooked by them rather like a concerned observer. Graham said that he could see the usefulness of the idea but thought it would be difficult when tired or upset. The therapist suggested that at these particular times he might deliberately intensify the thoughts/images to test out whether they really have any power.

Seventh to tenth interviews

The structure of the last sessions is shown in Table 8.6.

By the seventh session Graham reported that though he had improved greatly in the speed of processing new motorcycles to be sold, he still spent an inordinately long time on preparing vintage motorcycles for sale. Graham reasoned that manufacturers of new motorcycles will most likely have done their own checks recently, so the responsibility was theirs but that was not the case with vintage machines. The therapist reminded Graham of the

Table 8.5 Fourth to sixth interviews

1. Review of homework, re-assessment
2. Detached mindfulness
3. Exposure and response prevention
4. Distilling realistic estimates of threat and avoiding catastrophising, MOOD chart
5. Losing the fear of images/thoughts by deliberately increasing their intensity
6. Further behavioural experiments
7. Homework

Table 8.6 Seventh to tenth interviews

1. Review of homework
2. Tackling outstanding obsessions and compulsions
3. Acting as if intrusions are invalid. Use urge to ritualise as cue to exaggerate intrusions. Prevent rituals to test invalidity of intrusions. Expose self to obsessional stimuli while abandoning rituals
4. Construction of own self-help manual, coping with setbacks
5. Re-assessment and follow-up

importance of making realistic probability estimates and in this context asked him that given the low power of a vintage motorcycle and that they were coveted by older users, what was the likelihood of an accident with them. Graham agreed that it was probably less than his estimate of '1 in 1000' for the general machines he supplied. The therapist also reminded Graham of the importance of addressing the chances of 'catastrophic outcomes' with the old machines and Graham agreed that because of the low speeds of the older machine a rider would most likely get some early warning that something was not right and stop to investigate. The final sessions are a consolidation of the earlier sessions, with the last session taking place a month after the previous one to ensure gains are maintained and providing the opportunity to trouble-shoot any residual difficulties. By the tenth session Graham's Y-BOC score was 10 – in the normal region. The therapeutic focus then became relapse prevention and Graham was invited to 'build' a survival manual:

THERAPIST: Just as there are probably manuals that can serve as a reminder as to how to put together a vintage motorcycle, so if you have had no OCD symptoms for a time you may have forgotten how to get you functioning again and will need your own manual.

GRAHAM (laughing): I hope you are not implying I am 'vintage', no I take your point I don't want to be thrashing about like a headless chicken.

THERAPIST: You might want to put a picture of a 'headless chicken' on the cover of your Survival Manual! the idea is to make it your own. I would like to go through the 'Recovered but . . .' form to highlight the important areas that need to be covered.

GRAHAM: Looking at the first item my Achilles heel is getting stressed out, that is when I check more.

THERAPIST: So you could put stress as a trigger under item 1 and checking as a warning sign under item 3; what about item 2, the thinking that comes on stream when you go into OCD mode?

GRAHAM: I don't think it is so much my thinking that is the problem, it is more taking seriously this gremlin in my head that commands me to check. Though I suppose I am saying 'I must obey the gremlin', that could go under item 2.

THERAPIST: Maybe you should see yourself as a new army recruit intent on subordination and do a drawing of yourself as a recruit in the manual.

GRAHAM: I always fancied insubordination when I was in the Territorial Army but never dared.

THERAPIST: Now is your opportunity, you could put insubordination under item 4 and even if you delay responding to a command it is a start.

GRAHAM: Looking at some of the reminders on the form I am going to have to watch my perfectionism and I am going to have to remind myself that perfectionism is inefficient, it's magical thinking for me to think if I have everything perfect nothing bad will happen.

THERAPIST: Maybe don't try too hard to get the manual right, you can update it as you go along; trying too hard is a key problem with OCD.

GRAHAM: There are regular updates of motorcycle manuals; I probably need to update my 'service' manual every now and again, maybe make it available to others on the web see if it helps them.

THERAPIST: Great idea, could form a support group around it.

The above extract also highlights that cognitive restructuring can take place not only by tackling discrete individual thoughts, using devices such as the MOOD record, but also by the use of metaphors, 'gremlins', 'insubordinate army recruit' and 'motorcycle maintenance' that are personally relevant to the client.

Chapter 9

Generalised anxiety disorder

The hallmarks of generalised anxiety disorder (GAD) are persistent uncontrollable worry about a wide range of matters and vigilance for threat. Two-thirds of GAD sufferers have an onset between age 11 and their early twenties with usually no particular trigger but a significant minority have an onset in middle adulthood generally associated with a major life-event such as the death of a loved one. The amygdala and the ventrolateral prefrontal cortex constitute a neural circuit that is responsible for the detection of threats. Young people with GAD have been found to have hyperactivation of the amygdala that is not moderated by the actions of the ventrolateral prefrontal cortex (Monk *et al.* 2008).

Whilst 17.7% of psychiatric outpatients suffer from GAD, their main reason for seeking treatment is usually because of some co-morbid disorder (the commonest associated disorders are social phobia 34.7%, depression 22.2% and OCD 12.5%) (Zimmerman *et al.* 2008). However, the development of GAD often precedes the development of depression; put simply the sufferer may get 'fed up' being anxious.

Diagnosis

Diagnosis of GAD in DSM-IV-TR (American Psychiatric Association 2000) requires that the person has worried uncontrollably about a wide range of matters, more days than not in the past 6 months, and has at least three of seven symptoms. Enquiries about each of the symptoms can be made using the questions on the GAD page of the Pocketbook (Appendix D). The symptoms are also embodied in the GAD-7 Scale (Spitzer *et al.* 2006), in which clients rate answers (0 = not at all, 1 = several days, 2 = more than half the days, 3 = nearly every day) to the seven DSM-IV defined GAD symptoms: how often in the past 2 weeks they felt (1) nervous, anxious, or on edge; (2) easily annoyed or irritable; (3) afraid as if something awful might happen; (4) worried about different things; (5) restless and unable to sit still; (6) unable to stop or control worrying; and (7) trouble relaxing. Scores of 5, 10 and 15 represent cutpoints for mild, moderate and severe anxiety, respectively. (The GAD-7 is freely available on the internet for personal use, www.mhchoice.csip.org.uk). The GAD-7 is so brief that clients can be asked to complete it for homework after each session (for weekly sessions the time frame would need to be altered to the past week as opposed to 'the past 2 weeks'), to monitor progress without any fear of overburdening them.

Outcome of CBT treatments for GAD

The earlier studies of the effect of CBT on GAD focused variously on applied relaxation, anxiety management or the application of Beck's model of anxiety (Beck *et al.* 1985). The results were modest with about 50% of sufferers achieving high end state functioning. However, with advances in theorising and refinement in treatment Ladouceur *et al.* (2000) found three out of four clients were free of GAD at the end of treatment and at one year follow-up. White *et al.* (1992) evaluated a purely didactic CBT programme for generalised anxiety disorder. Treatment consisted of groups of 20 or more clients attending six 2-hour 'evening classes' for 'stress control'. Clients were told that no personal problems were to be discussed. Although there was no individual CBT control group, the results of the large group programme were comparable to those found in GAD programmes up to that time and it was judged more cost-effective. Interestingly in a comparison of individual and group CBT for GAD, Dugas *et al.* (2003) found that both were equally effective and produced very positive outcomes for approximately two-thirds of clients with GAD.

Cognitive behavioural models of GAD

The cognitive behavioural model of GAD depicted in Figure 9.1 is an amalgam of that of Wells (1997) and that of Dugas *et al.* (2007).

In Figure 9.1 uncontrollable/problematic worry is maintained by the five 'orbiting planets'; the relative importance of the 'planets' and their relationship with each other has only been partially elaborated:

1 *Conflicting appraisals of worry*. Wells (1997) has suggested that there are two types of worry. Type one worry is a worry about content, e.g. 'I am worried about passing this exam', and type two worry refers to negative appraisal of worrying itself (meta-worry), e.g. 'if I go on worrying like this I am going to put myself in an early grave'. He suggests that GAD sufferers have both positive beliefs about worry, e.g. 'if I don't worry something bad will happen', and negative beliefs; operating on these simultaneously serves to perpetuate worry.

2 *Rigid positive beliefs about the usefulness of worrying*. Wells (1997) has also suggested that positive beliefs about the benefits of worrying are

Figure 9.1 Cognitive behavioural model of GAD.

held with greater rigidity by GAD sufferers, e.g. 'if I didn't worry it would mean I don't care and that would be terrible'.

3   *Intolerance of uncertainty.* Dugas *et al.* (2007) found that intolerance of uncertainty along with negative problem orientation were the major predictors of severity of GAD. Approaching the same problem from a slightly different angle, Wells (1997) has suggested that GAD sufferers are excessively focused (monitoring) on their mental/physical state, evaluate it with maladaptive meta-cognitions, e.g. 'I have got to know that he/she has arrived safely', and thereby pursue inappropriate goal states, e.g. the feeling of certainty. Thus intolerance of uncertainty within Wells' model would be a special case of a more general problem of maladaptive meta-cognitions.

4   *Negative problem orientation.* Dugas *et al.* (2007) have suggested that although GAD sufferers are not deficient in problem solving skills per se, i.e. given an already defined problem they can solve it as well as anyone, they do have a deficit in problem orientation, i.e. they do not see discrete problems, deal in generalities, e.g. 'it's all too much', and consequently do not lock on to problems.

5   *Cognitive/behavioural/emotional avoidance.* Dugas *et al.* (2007) have suggested that the GAD sufferers use cognitive avoidance, i.e. they block the answering of anxiogenic questions, e.g. what if I fail this exam? This applies to images as well as thoughts, e.g. 'I replace threatening mental

images with things I say to myself in my mind'. In addition Wells (1997) has posited that behavioural avoidance, e.g. busying oneself tidying at an intrusive anxiogenic thought, and emotional avoidance, e.g. avoiding the feeling of helplessness by trying to control others' behaviour, 'control freak', also serve to maintain problematic worry.

Case formulation

A case formulation connects diagnosis to treatment. The 'casenness' represents a specific example of a cognitive model of a disorder. A comprehensive account of a client's difficulties also requires a specification of vulnerabilities, precipitants and perpetuating factors. Further from a treatment perspective it is also important to specify the client's strengths so that these may be capitalised on in therapy. The steps to be followed in a case formulation are illustrated with respect to a client, Tina.

1. Diagnosis. Tina was diagnosed as suffering from generalised anxiety disorder and social phobia, by directly accessing the symptoms in the DSM-IV-TR (American Psychiatric Association 2000) diagnostic sets for these disorders using the Pocketbook (Appendix D). She also scored 16 on the GAD-7 (Spitzer *et al.* 2006), which placed her just within the severe region. Tina also completed the Anxious Thoughts Inventory (AnTI, Wells 1994), which has three subscales: social worries, health worries and meta-worries. She scored highly on the social worries subscale, endorsing items such as 'I worry about saying or doing the wrong thing when among strangers', and the meta-worries subscale, endorsing items such as 'I worry that I cannot control my thoughts as well as I would like to', but endorsed few items on the health worries subscale.

2. Vulnerabilities. Tina lost her father in a road traffic accident when she was 10; the news was broken to her by a neighbour who was asked to look after her whilst her mother was at the hospital. She reported that she had been very close to her father. Tina suffered from bed wetting for about 3 months afterwards and her sleep was disturbed for the same period. She also remembered being clingy and bad-tempered for about a year afterwards. Though it was not diagnosed at the time she probably suffered from separation anxiety disorder for about a year afterwards, making her more vulnerable to developing anxiety problems later in life. She dated her tendency to worry from about age 11 and it had become progressively worse.

3. Precipitants. Tina presented to her GP in her late twenties concerned about her social phobia, which was affecting her performance at work. The GP noted that on the First Step Questionnaire she screened positive not only for social phobia but also for generalised anxiety disorder; further she wanted help for the latter as well. She was referred to a therapist who confirmed diagnoses of GAD and social phobia. There appeared to be no recent trigger for the GAD.

4. Protective factors.   Tina was very keen on exercising and had regularly gone to the gym/swimming until she had a flu bug 6 months previously and now attended spasmodically. The therapist hypothesised that a possible trigger for the full-blown GAD was the cessation of the regular exercise. Re-instituting the exercise became a therapeutic target, as it had probably previously protected her from GAD.

GAD Sat Nav

The GAD Sat Nav is presented in Table 9.1.

Tina felt that her worrying was uncontrollable and the therapist introduced her to the worry time strategy for pigeon-holing worries. It was explained that attempts to blank worrisome thought had the opposite effect but deciding to address them systematically at a fixed time (worry time) could stop her getting hooked by them. However, she was fearful that if she did not address the worries when they occurred something bad might happen. The therapist agreed that Tina might stay with the worrisome thoughts when they occurred long enough to determine the bottom line, and that it would be the latter that would be subjected to critical examination in the worry half hour. In order to determine the bottom line Tina was asked to repeatedly ask herself 'what is

Table 9.1 Generalised anxiety disorder Sat Nav

Therapeutic targets	Treatment strategies
1. Uncontrollable worry	Worry time
2. Perception that demands exceed resources	Behavioural experiment. Working sequentially rather than simultaneously, weaning off excessive responsibility – responsibility pie
3. Simultaneous positive and negative beliefs about worry	Challenging anxiogenic meta-cognitions about worry
4. Task interfering cognitions (TIC)	Switching to task oriented cognitions (TOC) TIC/TOC, problem solving
5. Tension	Relaxation exercises, exercise
6. Intolerance of uncertainty	The certainty of uncertainty – the futility of intolerance A fear that it is not necessary to be afraid of
7. Relapse prevention	Personally constructed self-help 'manual', utilising key points from therapy and drawing on self-help books and computer assisted material

so bad about that?' (the downward arrow technique) in response to each worrisome thought, thereby arriving at the 'core' of her problem. Further the therapist said that just thinking through a worrisome thought long enough to identify the bottom line was in itself a behavioural experiment, in which she was testing out whether such proscribed thinking had any dire consequences. However, as the therapist was writing this down as a homework exercise, Tina exclaimed that it was 'all too much'. The therapist was briefly stuck for a response but, glancing at the Sat Nav (Table 9.1), was cued to explain that the perception that a task was beyond her resources was characteristic of patients with GAD, adding that it was possible to bridge the expectation–experience gap by the realisation that this was a game Tina was inadvertently playing on herself. To become mindful of this game, Tina could rate how fearful she was on a scale 0–10 (where 10 was maximum anxiety) in anticipation of the worry time exercise and how fearful she was when she actually did it. The differing numbers could then be used as a reminder to help defuse situations where she was markedly apprehensive.

Tina was concerned that she was passing on her anxieties to her eight-year-old daughter, who was now refusing to attend Morris dancing. She had she believed encouraged her daughter's dancing but the latter was worrying about her performance so much that she now wanted to give it up. Tina felt she could see herself in her daughter worrying about matters so much to get things right but at the same time feeling her worrying was destructive. The therapist explained that she was trapped by the combination of her positive beliefs about worry and her negative beliefs about the consequences. Using her daughter as a model the therapist suggested that if her daughter was encouraged to relinquish her rigidly held positive belief about performing perfectly in favour of 'worrying' to the extent of a 'generally good enough' performance, sometimes falling below this benchmark sometimes above, then matters would be much easier. In the same way she could escape from her trap by forgoing her perfectionism.

The therapist suggested to Tina that she try explaining to her daughter that she had little 'gremlins' in her head that would constantly mock her: 'You are not up to this. Who do you think you are? Everyone will think you are stupid?' and she needed to tell them to 'take a hike' and just concentrate on the next task, visualising doing it well. Tina was enthusiastic about this and the therapist explained that the adult version of the 'gremlins' were TICs (task interfering cognitions) and that staying on task involved TOCs (task oriented cognitions) and that her worry would not become problematic if she remembered the mnemonic TIC/TOC to switch her stream of thought to a problem solving mode. The TICs/'gremlins' were representative of a negative problem orientation. The therapist also suggested that Tina might teach her daughter a relaxation response for use immediately before performing, taking a deep breath, breathing out slowly saying r-e-l-a-x, dropping her jaw and shoulders. Further in a similar manner she herself might spend a few minutes a day tensing each muscle group for 5 seconds and releasing the tension in that group for 10 seconds, noticing the difference between tension and relaxation, her muscles becoming warm and the tension flowing out of her fingertips. Whilst Tina welcomed these suggestions she wanted assurance that 'my daughter will not turn out like me' and the therapist explained that she was winding herself up by not tolerating this uncertainty as no one could guarantee how their offspring matures. The focus then shifted onto the importance of a preparedness to always tolerate 'a small bag of uncertainty'.

Session by session programme

The procedures to be followed in the first interview have been described in Chapter 3. There now follows a session by session protocol for generalised anxiety disorder from session 2 onwards. The programme is based on those described by Wells (1997) and Dugas *et al.* (2007) and targets each of the 'planets' in Figure 9.1.

Second interview

The framework for the second interview is shown in Table 9.2.

Towards the end of the first interview the therapist presents a provisional case formulation. At the beginning of the second session the therapist recaps this model and invites comments and refinements from the client. Tina accepted that she had been a 'worrier' since the tragic death of her father when she was aged 10, and this had become more difficult when she had become self-conscious in social situations. She had been unable to date the onset of her social phobia but on reflection thought it was probably after she passed her part one Accountancy exams and was required to visit small businesses and do audits. The therapist used the downward arrow technique to ascertain the bottom line with regard to her social phobia:

THERAPIST: What is so bad about going out on site?
TINA: I will blush and stammer.

Table 9.2 Second interview

1. Review of provisional case formulations of each identified disorder
2. Review of overview of treatment strategies for a case of generalised anxiety disorder (pages 146–147 in *Moving On After Trauma*)
3. Review of cognitive, behavioural and emotional avoidance
4. Noting and postponing worries to a fixed time – worry time
5. Homework

THERAPIST: What is so bad about that?
TINA: I will be so embarrassed.
THERAPIST: What is so bad about that?
TINA: They will think I am a fraud.

The above example illustrates that the case formulation is not a once and for all event, it is subject to collaborative refinement. Tina worried excessively for days before going on site and was emotionally exhausted by the time she arrived. The therapist asked her to postpone these issues for consideration at a special time, in a worry half hour when she could address the issue of others thinking she is a 'fraud' and other issues such as the effect of her worrying on her daughter, in writing. Whilst some of the content of the writing was on social phobic concerns, the strategy of pigeon-holing worries is a key strategy for GAD, in this style the treatment of co-morbid disorders is integrated. Tina was given the rationale that 'half an hour's worry a day is more than enough for anyone' but Tina thought that much more was probably required and it was therefore agreed that she conduct a behavioural experiment to test whether there were any dire consequences from not doing more than 30 minutes worry a day. She felt encouraged in doing this by having read about a sufferer from GAD in *Moving On After Trauma* (Scott 2008: 146–147), and by reference to the case example the therapist stressed that noting and postponing an issue to a fixed time is very different to blocking the thought (cognitive avoidance) or trying to hurriedly distract oneself (behavioural avoidance); both these forms of avoidance intensify worry. The therapist recommended a 'detached-mindfulness' about worries noting them, not getting hooked and calmly pigeon-holing them.

Third and fourth interviews

The outline of the third and fourth sessions is shown in Table 9.3.

At the start of session 3, when asked by the therapist if there was anything she would like to put on the agenda, Tina replied 'being a control freak'. She

Table 9.3 Third and fourth interviews

1. Review of homework
2. Use of MOOD chart and common saboteurs:
   i. Overestimating danger
   ii. Underestimating resources
   iii. Catastrophising
   iv. A long 'what if . . .' chain
3. Relaxation exercise and exercise
4. Homework

said she realised this when she was doing her writing and explained that it affected her relationship with not only underlings at work but also with her daughter, and the therapist asked her to explain further:

TINA: I get home from work and then after having the evening meal with my daughter what do I do? I check through my finances instead of playing with her, how sad is that?

THERAPIST: What I would like to do is a slow motion action replay of such moments using the mood chart (Appendix E). Imagine you have just finished your evening meal; what thoughts would likely go through your mind?

TINA: I have got to get the finances done.

THERAPIST: OK, we can write that in the second column 'Observe thinking'. But I would like to clarify this thinking further, you have got to get the finances done because . . .?

TINA: Because I would be letting my daughter down.

THERAPIST: So you need to do them every night?

TINA: Well no, but I am afraid.

THERAPIST: Of what?

TINA: Ending up on the street.

THERAPIST: How much danger is there of that?

TINA: None really, I suppose it goes back to after my father died; money was tight then.

THERAPIST: Did you end up on the street?

TINA: No, but I remember being fearful of asking for things.

THERAPIST: It is almost as if it's the young Tina getting frightened, over-estimating the danger in the present situation and producing a catastrophic image. Going back to the framework of the MOOD chart what could you put for a more objective way of thinking that might comfort the young Tina?

TINA: I would tell her that there is no real danger, 'mummy' can always sort something out.

THERAPIST: I like that, it is really like comforting your daughter and you would need to do it as much with hugs, say hugging a cushion as with words. But then in the final column of the MOOD chart you would need to move on; what would you put there?

TINA: I could do something like play with my daughter or spend 10 minutes on my exercise bike.

THERAPIST: Regular exercise is great for GAD sufferers; afterwards problems do not seem quite as large, it is like you start looking through the right end of the binoculars.

TINA: I did buy some relaxation tapes but somehow when I try to relax I get more wound up.

THERAPIST: You do get relaxation-induced anxiety in a minority of people with applied relaxation strategies and you are probably better with the regular use of the exercise bike.

The above extract highlights the role that developmental problems can have and the need to address them not only at the adult level of realistic thinking about danger, and resources but also in a developmentally appropriate manner. Further GAD is not a purely intra-psychic phenomenon, it has bodily accompaniments and these ought also to be addressed in therapy.

At the start of the fourth interview Tina reported progress on becoming less of a 'control freak' and was delegating more tasks at work. However the downside was that it was playing on her mind as she tried to get to sleep – she would embark on a long 'what if . . .?' chain: 'What if I rely on the spreadsheet my colleague has supplied? What if the organisation complains? What if my boss complains? What if I get sacked?' The therapist explained the importance of keeping the chain as short as possible, answering each 'what if?' before proceeding to the next. It was agreed that Tina would check the accuracy of one in ten of her colleague's spreadsheets to give her reasonable confidence in their accuracy thereby circumventing other worst case scenarios.

Fifth and sixth interviews

The outline of the fifth and sixth interviews is shown in Table 9.4.

At re-assessment in the fifth session Tina score 11 on the GAD-7. Thus although there had been a clinically significant improvement in her condition she was still moderately anxious. She had found it difficult to accept scrutinising just one in ten of her colleague's spreadsheets and felt that she had to 'know' that each was right. The therapist emphasised that it was important to target one of the 'planets' that maintain worry, 'intolerance of uncertainty' if she was to continue to delegate. Tina added that one colleague to whom she delegated a task became irate with her as she stood over her watching her manipulate columns of figures on the computer screen. The therapist suggested that she was having a battle between her task interfering cognitions (TICs), 'nobody else will do it properly', and task orientated cognitions (TOCs), 'delegation is necessary if I am to avoid being overloaded', and that she needed to switch from one to the other TIC/TOC.

Table 9.4 Fifth and sixth interviews

1. Review of homework, re-assessment
2. Task interfering cognitions (TICs) and task oriented cognitions (TOCs), TIC/TOC, problem solving
3. Intolerance of uncertainty
4. Negative problem orientation
5. Homework

At the sixth session Tina had noted on her MOOD chart that her mood had taken a dip on a Sunday afternoon thinking about work the next day. The chart further indicated that she had dealt with this observed dip by getting on her exercise bike and nothing had been written in the objective thinking column. The therapist pointed that the gap in the MOOD chart had arisen because of emotional avoidance; instead of staying with the feeling of apprehension on the Sunday afternoon and sorting out how well founded it was she had blocked the emotion, jumping to column four. Tina agreed that the benefits of the bike on the Sunday afternoon were indeed short-lived. (The therapist reiterated that each form of avoidance, emotional, cognitive and behavioural, serves to maintain worry.) Approaching this incident from a slightly different angle the therapist suggested that on Sunday afternoon Tina had failed to 'lock on' to a problem and that this failure to lock on to problems is quite characteristic of GAD sufferers. The therapist explained that it was rather like one of her underlings not preparing a spreadsheet for her and going off sick instead of saying which part of the Excel program they were stuck with. Tina could appreciate that only if a problem was owned and defined could it be solved. Interestingly in her first line management training Tina had been introduced to the steps of problem solving (defining a problem carefully, 'no fuzzies', brainstorming solutions, going for quality not quantity, looking at the advantages and disadvantages of each solution short and long term, choosing a solution, planning and implementing the solution, reviewing the solution in the light of experience, trying another solution if necessary) but no one had told her about the importance of the very first step, problem orientation.

Seventh to ninth interviews

The outline of the seventh to ninth interviews is shown in Table 9.5.

At the seventh session Tina felt she had become more adept at problem orientation but sometimes she had not been able to complete the problem solving process. She had discovered that about half the spreadsheets of one colleague were wrong and had felt torn between not wanting to appear a control freak but not wanting to delegate any more. At this juncture the therapist introduced her to the information processing biases (see Table 4.2) and suggested that she was sabotaging the problem solving process by using

Table 9.5 Seventh to ninth interviews

1. Review of homework
2. Saboteurs to problem solving
3. Examining the validity, utility and authority for beliefs (both positive and negative) about worry
4. Behavioural experiments
5. Homework including compilation of survival manual

dichotomous thinking, 'either I am a control freak or I delegate'. On inspecting Table 4.2 Tina also suggested that she was personalising matters in assuming that just because something had gone wrong it must be her fault. It was agreed that whenever she delegated a new task to a person she should always build in a review and expect that usually new learning will be incomplete. For homework Tina was asked to be vigilant for the saboteurs of the problem solving process.

In the eighth session the therapist introduced Tina to cross-examining her positive and negative beliefs about worry using the matrix in Table 9.6.

Tina brought along a completed Table 9.6 to the ninth session and was struck that her authority for her positive beliefs about the benefit of worry was in fact her mother and that it was her own (Tina's) beliefs about the negative consequences of worry that she was operating on rather than any scientific evidence. Tina found however that she was still having long post-mortems about how well she had performed at staff meetings and she was encouraged to conduct a behavioural experiment by pigeon-holing these concerns for her worry time and see whether this led to any decrement in performance at the next meeting. Within the worry time she could also consider the material she had been taught for her co-morbid social phobia. In addition for homework Tina was asked to write her own survival manual.

Tenth to twelfth interviews

The outline of the tenth to twelfth sessions is shown in Table 9.7.

By the tenth session Tina scored 4 on the GAD-7, which is the normal region, and endorsed no maladaptive meta-cognitions on the Anxious

Table 9.6 Challenging positive and negative beliefs about worry

	Validity How true?	Utility How useful?	Authority Who says?
Positive beliefs about worry, e.g. it shows I care			
Negative beliefs about worry, e.g. I am going to damage my health if I carry on worrying			

Table 9.7 Tenth to twelfth interviews

1. Review of homework, re-assessment
2. Trouble shooting difficulties using problem solving framework
3. Refining survival manual

Thoughts Inventory (Wells 1997). It was stressed by the therapist that worry was such a lifelong habit with Tina that it was unrealistic to think that there would never again be times when it would become problematic and an appropriate focus for the remaining sessions was relapse prevention. Further, given that she had also suffered from social phobia and recovered, it would be fitting to apply the relapse prevention training framework also to the social phobia. The therapist introduced 'Recovered but . . .', Appendix I, as a lens with which Tina could focus her efforts in the construction of a survival manual and it was suggested the latter should also include her homework assignments and highlight any self-help materials she had found useful. As such, it was a question of 'when' she would have to use her manual rather than 'if'. The therapist first addressed item 1 in 'Recovered but . . .':

THERAPIST: What do you think might trigger uncontrollable worry in the future?

TINA: Perhaps my daughter staying overnight at friends or going away with the school.

THERAPIST: So that could go under item 1; what might trigger the social phobia?

TINA: Having to give a presentation in work.

THERAPIST: What sort of internal dialogue would you have with yourself if your daughter was away from you?

TINA: I should be there for her, she won't be able to cope.

THERAPIST: That could go under item 2; what could you put as a better way of thinking in these situations?

TINA: I suspect I won't even try a better way of thinking like the 'objective thinking' on the MOOD chart, I'll just go for avoiding uncontrollable worry by not letting her go on these adventures.

THERAPIST: Is this what you really want?

TINA: No, not really, she has to have adventures to grow up, I'm not going to be here for ever, it's not fair for me to hold her back.

THERAPIST: So the real enemy that you should put under item 2 is emotional avoidance with thoughts such as 'I must avoid worry at all costs'.

TINA: I am forever saying 'all I want is a bit of peace', but I have realised that is part of my problem pursuing an unrealistic goal.

THERAPIST: Well maybe put that under item 4, 'pursue realistic goals'.

TINA: I think that is also a problem with getting anxious about presentations. I am wanting to be relaxed before and during. Then when I am not I think others will pick it up and be critical of me.

THERAPIST: Maybe in your survival manual draw a sea with some waves and yourself swimming in those conditions, then a totally calm pool but you sinking beneath the surface with arms outstretched as a reminder.

TINA: Those pictures give me something more concrete to hang onto, I'll draw and colour them to make them more memorable.

The above extract indicates how not only homework materials for different disorders can be addressed simultaneously but so too can relapse prevention materials. Further it is not necessary to restrict cognitive restructuring to the cross-examination of individual negative thoughts but the restructuring can also take place via imagery/metaphor. Finally, by helping Tina to focus through the lens of items 5 to 8 of Appendix I, the therapist was able to reframe her goal as stopping worry significantly interfering with her life as opposed to stopping worrying.

Chapter 10

Putting it all together

The previous six chapters have detailed disorder-specific cognitive conceptualisations which have informed the choice of therapeutic interventions. The treatment protocols for the different disorders considered in Chapters 4 to 9 have certain commonalities (Table 10.1).

Further all clients travel the Simply Effective pathway (Fig. 10.1).

Whilst there is an invariable structure to treatment sessions and assessment, the content of sessions varies by disorder. This variation is apparent in the different Sat Navs, Appendix D, for the different disorders. The clarity of the session by session agendas makes it possible to determine whether a client has had CBT treatment for a disorder from which they are suffering and also to determine whether any additional disorder has been addressed. Therapist competence can be screened using the series of questions in Table 10.2 (reproduced in Appendix G):

Positive answers to each of the five questions probably indicate an at least minimally acceptable level of competence. The Therapist Competence Screen addresses fidelity to a treatment protocol; without fidelity it is impossible to know whether the specified treatment works. Importantly the first question

Table 10.1 Commonalities in the treatment of the common disorders

1. Treatment is active, directive and time limited
2. Treatment is directed by the interplay of diagnosis and case formulation
3. Treatment stresses independent use of strategies outside the therapy session
4. Treatment targets key cognitions (thoughts and images) and behaviours
5. Clients are encouraged to see improvements as a consequence of their behaviour
6. A psycho-educational approach is adopted that involves the setting and review of homework
7. Therapist and client are collaborators conducting behavioural experiments to test out negative predictions
8. Cognitive restructuring takes place not only by Socratic questioning but also by the use of metaphor
9. Special attention is given to the client staying well by the construction of an individualised survival manual

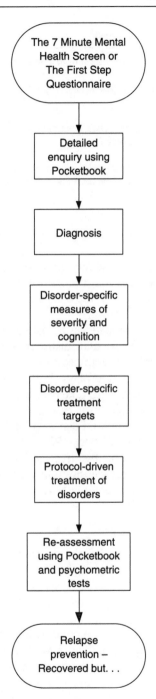

Figure 10.1 The simply effective pathway.

Table 10.2 Therapist Competence Screen

1. Did the therapist collaborate with the client in addressing his/her pressing concerns?
   Yes   No
2. Did the therapist focus on a therapeutic target appropriate for the disorder (first column in Sat Nav)?
   Yes   No
3. Did the therapist employ an appropriate treatment strategy for the targeted problem (second column in Sat Nav)?
   Yes   No
4. Did the therapist negotiate a homework assignment that addressed the therapeutic target and integrated new learning from the session?
   Yes   No   Unsure
5. Was there a review of homework?
   Yes   No

on the Screen makes it clear that fidelity does not involve a slavish focus on a treatment target but underlines that it is critical to enter a client's here and now before using the contents of these concerns to illustrate a treatment strategy.

A supervisor may assess competence by asking a supervisee to role play a particular session for a particular disorder, rating performance using Table 10.2. The transcripts of therapy sessions in this volume are vignettes that can be used to construct role plays. Part of a transcript may be first modelled, then the student invited to take over the therapeutic role and given feedback. Alternatively the supervisor can assess a video/audio tape of an actual therapy session. Such material can also be rated using the Cognitive Therapy Rating Scale (Young and Beck 1980) but this scale (with the exception of depression) does not assess treatment fidelity, although it does importantly assess general therapeutic skills, e.g. empathy, warmth, and specific cognitive skills, e.g. Socratic questioning.

Some reminders and tips

For more detailed explanation of the reminders/tips see the indicated chapters.

Chapters 1, 2 and 3

1   Over half the cases of common mental health problems are missed; this can be prevented by screening (The 7 Minute Mental Health Screen or First Step Questionnaire) and directly asking questions about each of the symptoms in a diagnostic set (the CBT Pocketbook, Appendix D).
2   Clients want help with all the disorders from which they are suffering not just the main disorder with which they present.

3 A diagnosis indicates which cognitive model is pertinent, whilst a case formulation represents a specific example of a cognitive model.

4 A case formulation is developed by eliciting predisposing factors, precipitating factors, perpetuating factors and protective factors.

5 KISS (Keep It Simple Stupid) – keep therapy simple, include metaphor and simple diagrams.

6 Focus on SMART: specific, measurable, achievable and realistic targets.

7 Remain faithful to the CBT protocol for the disorder(s) but with flexibility.

8 Always enter the client's here and now and generally use this to illustrate new teaching.

9 The structuring of sessions and the setting/review of homework are likely to be important predictors of how much the client benefits from treatment. Without written homework assignments it is very difficult to judge adherence.

10 The client's reality is usually of suffering from more than one disorder; focus on each disorder within a session and assign homework pertinent to each disorder.

11 There is no evidence that 'generic' (i.e. without a diagnosis) CBT works.

12 Include a measure of the severity of the disorder(s) and a measure that assesses cognitions that are pertinent to the disorder(s).

13 The PHQ-9 for depression and GAD-7 for generalised anxiety disorder are so brief that clients with these disorders can easily complete them after each session for homework, allowing for careful tracking of progress.

14 Psychometric tests are not a substitute for diagnosis; they tend to give many false positives, which can lead to a targeting of the wrong disorder.

15 Be open-minded about new developments in CBT, but ask what is the evidence that the new approach adds to the effectiveness of the standard approaches outlined in this volume? Beware of marketing and hopping from workshop to workshop.

16 Expect to get stuck sometimes in a therapy session; refer to the Pocketbook for help. Accept that learning a skill is largely about learning from mistakes.

17 Relapse prevention is an important ingredient of all the programmes. A multi-faceted approach is needed, embracing the construction of a survival manual, involvement of significant others, use of self-help books (e.g. *Feeling Good: The New Mood Therapy* and *Moving On After Trauma*) and computer assisted therapy (e.g. Mood Gym).

Chapter 4: Depression

18 Be aware of depression about depression which can arise because the person concludes that there are no justifying event(s). Ensure that there

are slow motion action replays of dips in mood using the MOOD chart.

19 Ensure that after tracking their mood and developing objective thinking, the depressed client does not engage in rumination but decides what to do and does it – the 'D' in the MOOD chart.

20 Assist the depressed client to make a broad investment portfolio as a long-term strategy for managing mood. But acknowledge that many tasks will have to be broken down into manageable sub-tasks.

Chapter 5: Panic disorder

21 Panic disorder is maintained by catastrophic cognitions and avoidance behaviour; both need to be targeted.

22 The catastrophic cognitions that play a pivotal role in the maintenance of panic attacks should be challenged not only verbally but also experientially by behavioural experiments, e.g. hyperventilation challenge.

23 Panic disorder clients with agoraphobic avoidance can be weaned off behavioural avoidance by daring them to gradually approach situations they have been avoiding and stay in situations that they have been escaping from.

Chapter 6: Post-traumatic stress disorder

24 The goal of treatment for post-traumatic stress disorder is to stop clients re-experiencing the trauma. Paradoxically this is achieved by a deliberate specific focus on the details of the trauma by variously writing about it, reading over an account out loud daily until the trauma is simply remembered.

25 PTSD treatment can be a challenge to the therapeutic alliance in that clients are committed to blocking the memory, whilst the therapist is suggesting confronting the memory; the impasse can be resolved by focusing on 'better ways' of handling the traumatic memory.

26 Dare PTSD clients to gradually tackle what they have been avoiding.

27 Social support is the biggest predictor of recovery from PTSD and a family member/friend of the client should if possible be asked to attend at least some of the sessions.

Chapter 7: Social phobia

28 For clients with social phobia challenge the 'story' they have of others' evaluation of them as a consequence of their social interactions.

29 Encourage the client with social phobia to gradually encounter situations they fear.

Chapter 8: Obsessive compulsive disorder

30 Explain to OCD sufferers that their intrusive thoughts/images are normal; it is their attempts at neutralising them that leads to their persistent difficulties.

31 Dare the OCD sufferer to gradually postpone their repetitive behaviour and thereby test out whether there are any deleterious consequences.

32 Highlight for the OCD sufferer the link between low mood and compulsions, and teach mood management using the MOOD chart.

Chapter 9: Generalised anxiety disorder

33 For clients with generalised anxiety disorder make a distinction between problem solving and worrying/agonising, question the utility and function of the latter.

34 With GAD clients tackle the somatic symptoms, i.e. tension, irritability, poor sleep, by advocating exercise and relaxation exercises.

35 Be aware of magical thinking which may be present in PTSD, OCD and GAD and takes the form of 'if I check/worry then I can prevent . . .'. Teach the client to switch from the child magical thinking mode to adult mode.

Chapter 10: Putting it all together

36 There is a limit to the learning that can take place with a textbook. Seek opportunities to see therapy sessions demonstrated, then role play sessions with feedback and have some actual sessions taped or videoed for further feedback. Teaching that does not first demonstrate good practice is of doubtful utility and likely unnecessarily stressful.

37 Therapist competence involves not only identifying treatment targets and implementing matching treatment strategies but also (a) acknowledging a client's current pressing concerns and using them to illustrate important therapeutic points and (b) the setting and review of homework.

Readers may wish to discuss their experience of reading and implementing the material in this volume on the www.simplyeffectivecbt.com website, which will also contain additional materials and tips to aid the therapist.

Appendix A

Personality disorders and cognitive content

Cluster A personality disorders

1   Paranoid personality disorder. A pervasive distrust and suspiciousness of others such that their motives are interpreted as malevolent:

- 'Often people deliberately want to annoy me.'
- 'I cannot trust other people.'
- 'It isn't safe to confide in other people.'

2   Schizoid personality disorder. A pervasive pattern of detachment from social relationships and a restricted range of expressions of emotions in interpersonal settings:

- 'Relationships are messy and interfere with freedom.'
- 'Intimate relations with other people are not important to me.'
- 'I shouldn't confide in others.'

3   Schizotypal personality disorder. A pervasive pattern of social and interpersonal deficits marked by acute discomfort with, and reduced capacity for, close relationships as well as by cognitive or perceptual distortions and eccentricities of behaviour. Cognitive content is much the same as schizoid above.

Cluster B personality disorders

1   Antisocial personality disorder. A pervasive pattern of disregard and violation of the rights of others occurring since age 15:

- 'Other people are weak and deserve to be taken.'
- 'If I want something I should do whatever is necessary to get it.'
- 'People will get at me if I don't get at them first.'

2   Borderline personality disorder (BPD). A pervasive pattern of instability of interpersonal relationship, self-image, and affects, and marked impulsivity. The cognitive content of BPD (Butler *et al.* 2002) reflect themes of

dependency, helplessness distrust, fears of rejection/abandonment/losing emotional control and extreme attention-seeking behaviour.

3   Histrionic personality disorder. A pervasive pattern of excessive emotionality and attention seeking:

- 'Unless I entertain or impress people, I am nothing.'
- 'I should be the centre of attention.'
- 'People will pay attention only if I act in extreme ways.'

4   Narcissistic personality disorder. A pervasive pattern of grandiosity (in fantasy or behaviour), need for admiration, and lack of empathy:

- 'I don't have to be bound by rules that apply to other people.'
- 'If others don't respect my status they should be punished.'
- 'People have no right to criticise me.'

Cluster C personality disorders

1   Avoidant personality disorder. A pervasive pattern of social inhibition, feelings of inadequacy, and hypersensitivity to negative evaluation:

- 'If people get close to me they will discover the real me and reject me.'
- 'If I think or feel something unpleasant I should try to wipe it out or distract myself.'
- 'Unpleasant feelings will escalate and get out of control.'

2   Dependent personality disorder. A pervasive and excessive need to be taken care of that leads to submissive and clinging behaviour and fears of separation:

- 'I am needy and weak.'
- 'I need somebody around available at all times to help me carry out what I need to do in case something bad happens.'
- 'I need others to help me make decisions or tell me what to do.'

3   Obsessive compulsive personality disorder. A pervasive pattern of pre-occupation with orderliness, perfectionism, and mental and interpersonal control, at the expense of flexibility, openness and efficiency:

- 'It is important to do a perfect job on everything.'
- 'Details are extremely important.'
- 'I have to depend on myself to see that things get done.'

Appendix B
Screening questionnaire

Questionnaire – *please answer each question as best you can*

Name: Date:

Address:

d.o.b.

Telephone no:

Are you working?

What kind of work do you do?

What kind of work (if any) did you do in the past?

How do you spend your day?

How were things at school?

Did you have any particular problems at school? If you did what were they?

Do you have any qualifications? If so what are they?

What (if any) are the major problems you are having at the moment?
1.

2.

3.

Please indicate when the problems listed above began and also if there was a time when they got much worse.

1.

2.

3.

Have any very scary things happened to you or did you see such things happening to others? If so write them down below and put when they happened (include any abuse in childhood).

1.

2.

3.

Have you had any professional (doctor or counsellor) help for any of your difficulties? If you did please indicate when, for how long and by whom.

1.

2.

3.

Have your parents or brothers or sisters suffered with their nerves? If yes please indicate who and if you can what they suffered or are suffering from.

What has your mood been like?

How much have you been drinking alcohol in the past month?

Have you been taking any drugs? Please indicate any prescribed drugs as well as any other drugs that you may be taking.

1.

2.

Was there a time in the past when you took drugs that were *not* prescribed by your doctor? YES/NO

If yes to the above please indicate what drug/s you took, when and for how long.

1.

2.

Have you been in trouble with the law? YES/NO

Appendix C
The 7 Minute Mental Health Screen/Audit

This screen is an interview format for the First Step Questionnaire (Appendix H) and provides guidance on interpreting the latter. It covers the common mental disorders and positive findings can be investigated further by turning, where indicated, to the relevant page in the Cognitive Behaviour Therapy Pocketbook (Appendix D). If the focus is on auditing the effects of an intervention, the time frame for questions can be altered, e.g. last 2 weeks.

1. Depression	Yes	No	Don't know
During the past month have you often been bothered by feeling, depressed or hopeless?			
During the past month have you often been bothered by little interest or pleasure in doing things?			
Is this something with which you would like help?			

A positive response to at least one symptom question and the help question suggests that detailed enquiry be made, page 163

2. Panic disorder and agoraphobia	Yes	No	Don't know
Do you have unexpected panic attacks, a sudden rush of intense fear or anxiety?			
Do you avoid situations in which the panic attacks might occur?			
Is this something with which you would like help?			

A positive response to at least one symptom question and the help question suggests that detailed enquiry be made, page 169

3. Post-traumatic stress disorder In your life, have you ever had any experience that was so frightening, horrible or upsetting that, in the past month, you	Yes	No	Don't know
i. Have had nightmares about it or thought about it when you did not want to?			
ii. Tried hard not to think about it or went out of your way to avoid situations that reminded you of it?			
iii. Were constantly on guard, watchful, or easily startled?			
iv. Felt numb or detached from others, activities, or your surroundings?			
Is this something with which you would like help?			

A positive response to at least three symptom questions and the help question suggests that detailed enquiry be made, pages 171–172

4. Generalised anxiety disorder	Yes	No	Don't know
Are you a worrier?			
Do you worry about everything?			
Has the worrying been excessive (more days than not) or uncontrollable in the last 6 months (a time frame of the last 2 weeks can be used if the intent is to audit an intervention rather than screen)?			
Is this something with which you would like help?			

A positive response to the two symptom questions and the help question suggests that detailed enquiry be made, page 165

5. Social phobia	Yes	No	Don't know
When you are or might be in the spotlight say in a group of people or eating/writing in front of others do you immediately get anxious or nervous?			
Do you avoid social situations out of a fear of embarrassing or humiliating yourself?			
Is this something with which you would like help?			

A positive response to at least one symptom question and the help question suggests that detailed enquiry be made, page 174

6. Obsessive compulsive disorder	Yes	No	Don't know
Are you bothered by thoughts, images or impulses that keep going over in your mind?			
Do you try to block these thoughts, images or impulses by thinking or doing something?			
Is this something with which you would like help?			

A positive response to the symptom questions and the help question suggests that detailed enquiry be made, page 167

7. Bulimia	Yes	No	Don't know
Do you go on binges where you eat very large amounts of food in a short period?			
Do you do anything special, such as vomiting, go on a strict diet to prevent gaining weight from the binge?			
Is this something with which you would like help?			

A positive response to the symptom questions and the help question suggests that detailed enquiry be made.

8. Substance abuse/dependence	Yes	No	Don't know
Have you felt you should cut down on your alcohol/drug?			
Have people got annoyed with you about your drinking/drug taking?			
Have you felt guilty about your drinking/drug use?			
Do you drink/use drugs before midday?			
Is this something with which you would like help?			

A positive response to at least two of the symptom questions and the help question suggests that detailed enquiry be made.

9. Psychosis	Yes	No	Don't know
Do you ever hear things other people don't hear, or see things they don't see?			
Do you ever feel like someone is spying on you or plotting to hurt you?			
Do you have any ideas that you don't like to talk about because you are afraid other people will think you are crazy?			
Is this something with which you would like help?			

A positive response to at least one of the symptom questions and the help question suggests that detailed enquiry be made.

10. Mania/hypomania	Yes	No	Don't know
Have there been times, lasting at least a few days, when you were unusually high, talking a lot, sleeping little?			
Did others notice that there was something different about you? If you answered 'yes', what did they say?			
Is this something with which you would like help?			

A positive response to at least one of the symptom questions and the help question suggests that detailed enquiry be made.

IMPORTANT NOTE: If when you inspect the 7 Minute Mental Health Screen or the First Step Questionnaire the person screened positive for either items 1 (depression), 8 (substance abuse/dependence), 9 (psychosis) or 10 (mania) ask:

Have you been hurting or making plans for hurting yourself?

Appendix D
Cognitive Behaviour Therapy Pocketbook

The disorders are listed in alphabetical order. For each disorder there are questions which directly access each symptom in the DSM-IV-TR criteria. For a symptom to be regarded as present it must produce clinically significant distress or impairment. When there is a need to re-assess the client, the same questions can be asked again to check progress.

A conceptualisation of each disorder is presented for sharing with the client. A Sat Nav for that disorder follows, to be used as an aide-memoire during therapy (it is not intended to replace the session by session guidelines). Finally usage of the Pocketbook is governed by the mnemonic FACT. The F and A stand for first assess. The third letter of FACT, 'C', stands for conceptualisation. The last letter of FACT, 'T', stands for treatment and under this heading the core cognitive behavioural interventions are summarised in the Sat Nav.

Depression

During the last 2 weeks:

1 Have you been sad, down or depressed most of the day nearly every day?
2 Have you lost interest or do you get less pleasure from the things you used to enjoy?
3 Have you been eating much less or much more?
4 Have you been having problems falling asleep, staying asleep or waking up too early of a morning?
5 Have you been fidgety, restless, unable to sit still or talking or moving more slowly than is normal for you?
6 Have you been tired all the time nearly every day?
7 Have you been bothered by feelings of worthlessness or guilt?
8 Have you had problems taking in what you are reading, watching/listening to or in making decisions about everyday things?
9 Have you been hurting or making plans for hurting yourself?

If the client answered yes to five or more of the above (at least one of which has to be question 1 or 2) then it is likely that the client is suffering from depression.

Conceptualisation – present a story that makes sense to the client and is consistent with the CBT model. Examples:

(a) 'on strike for better pay and conditions'
(b) 'stopped investing so there can't be a return'
(c) 'you equated your worth with doing . . . how do you know there can't be other routes to a sense of achievement and pleasure?'
(d) 'why would the dice be forever loaded against you?'

Depression Sat Nav

Therapeutic targets	Treatment strategies
1. Depression about depression	Focus on responsibility for working on solutions and not on responsibility for problem
2. Inactivity	Developing a broad investment portfolio, wide-ranging modest investments
3. Negative views of self, personal world and future	Challenging the validity, utility and authority by which these views are held. Use of MOOD chart
4. Information processing biases	Highlighting personal biases and stepping around them using MOOD chart
5. Overvalued roles	Valuing multiple roles, renegotiation of roles in social context
6. Relapse prevention	Personally constructed self-help 'manual', utilising key points from therapy and drawing on self-help books and computer assisted material

Generalised anxiety disorder

Ask the client if they would regard themselves as a 'worrier', in the sense that they always find something to worry about and if they are not worrying they worry that they are not worrying. If the worry has been excessive or uncontrollable (more days than not) for at least 6 months and they have three or more of the following symptoms (more days than not):

1   tiring very easily
2   restlessness, keyed up or on edge
3   difficulty concentrating or mind going blank
4   irritability
5   muscle tension
6   difficulty falling or staying asleep

then it is probable that they are suffering from generalised anxiety disorder. (However, a diagnosis of GAD is not given if they are suffering from depression; the latter is regarded as more significant in the diagnostic 'bible' DSM-IV-TR, American Psychiatric Association 2000).

Conceptualisation – the essence of GAD can be conveyed to clients as follows: 'worry about everything and nothing, worry even if there is nothing to worry about', 'imagination runs riot, what if this, what if that, what if the other'.

Generalised anxiety disorder Sat Nav

Therapeutic targets	Treatment strategies
1. Uncontrollable worry	Worry time
2. Perception that demands exceed resources	Behavioural experiment. Working sequentially rather than simultaneously, weaning off excessive responsibility – responsibility pie
3. Simultaneous positive and negative beliefs about worry	Challenging anxiogenic meta-cognitions about worry
4. Task interfering cognitions (TIC)	Switching to task oriented cognitions (TOC) TIC/TOC
5. Tension	Relaxation exercises, exercise
6. Intolerance of uncertainty	The certainty of uncertainty – the futility of intolerance. A fear that it is not necessary to be afraid of
7. Relapse prevention	Personally constructed self-help 'manual', utilising key points from therapy and drawing on self-help books and computer assisted material

Obsessive compulsive disorder

Obsessions

1   Are you bothered by thoughts, images or impulses that keep going over in your mind?
2   Do you try to block these thoughts, images or impulses by thinking or doing something?

Provided the client's concerns are not simply excessive worries about everyday problems and provided the client sees these thoughts, images as a product of his/her own mind, then yes responses to questions 1 and 2 above indicate a likely obsession.

Compulsions

1   Do you feel driven to repeat some behaviour, e.g. checking, washing, counting, or to repeat something in your mind over and over again to try to feel less comfortable?
2   If you do not do your special thing do you get very anxious?

Yes responses to these last two questions indicate a probable compulsion.

Note: the client has to be aware that their obsession and compulsion are excessive or irrational and they must also significantly interfere with functioning or cause significant distress.

Conceptualisation – normalise the client's thoughts/ideas/fantasies by likening the mind to a 'railway station', nobody can control what 'train of thought/image comes in'. Point out that (a) trying to neutralise them by overt behaviours, e.g. repeated handwashing, or covert rituals, e.g. counting to a certain number, 'feeds' the intrusions; (b) pursuing a feeling of certainty is like searching for the 'Holy Grail'; and (c) they take an excessive share of the 'responsibility pie'.

Obsessive compulsive disorder Sat Nav

Therapeutic targets	Treatment strategies
1. Model of mental life, thought–action fusion (TAF), attributing moral status to intrusions	Develop more appropriate model, decoupling fusion, emotional reasoning – the difference between feeling guilty and being guilty
2. Inappropriate goal state, e.g. absolute certainty, perfect cleanliness	Distilling achievable goals
3. Excessive responsibility	Responsibility pie
4. Bipolar functioning – perception of no choice (compulsion) alternating with perception of perfect freedom (leading to self-blame)	Encourage perception of reasonable degree of control by postponement strategies. Use of MOOD chart
5. Neutralising images, thoughts, behaviours	Exposure and response prevention. Behavioural experiments
6. Overestimation of danger	Distillation of realistic probabilities
7. Relapse prevention	Personally constructed self-help 'manual', utilising key points from therapy and drawing on self-help books and computer assisted material

Panic disorder and agoraphobia

1   Do you have times when you feel a sudden rush of intense fear that comes on, from out of the blue, for no reason at all?
2   Does it take less than ten minutes for the panic attack to reach its worst?
3   During your last bad panic attack did you have four or more of the following:

   i   Heart racing
   ii   Sweating
   iii Trembling or shaking
   iv Shortness of breath or smothering
   v   Feeling of choking
   vi   Chest pain
   vii Nausea
   viii Dizzy, light-headed, unsteady or faint
   ix   Things around seemed unreal
   x   Fear of losing control
   xi   Afraid you might die
   xii Numbness or tingling sensations
   xiii Chills or hot flushes

If the client answered yes to, each of the three questions above it is likely that they are suffering from panic disorder.

The client should then be asked: 'Some people with panic disorder avoid certain situations for fear of having a panic attack, e.g. going places alone, crowded shops; do you?' If this is the case it is then necessary to establish whether this avoidance interferes with their daily routine, job or social activities. If the answer to this is also yes then they are probably suffering from panic disorder with agoraphobic avoidance. The agoraphobic avoidance would be regarded as severe if they were totally unable to go out by themselves, mild if they just cannot go great distances by themselves and moderate if how far they can go by themselves is in between.

Conceptualisation

(a) *Advise that panic attacks are fuelled by catastrophic interpretation of unusual but not abnormal bodily sensations. View panic attacks as a 'Big Dipper Ride', ascending the symptoms get worse, tempting to get off near the top, but if the client does not do anything then the symptoms comes down the other side within ten minutes.*
(b) *Suggest that using 'safety behaviours' prevents learning that nothing terrible would happen if they did nothing at all in the panic situation.*

Panic disorder Sat Nav

Therapeutic targets	Treatment strategies
1. Catastrophising about bodily symptoms	Normalising bodily symptoms
2. Anxiety sensitivity	Induction of panic symptoms
3. Avoidance of feared situations	Graded exposure to feared situations
4. 'Safety' procedures	Daring to gradually wean off 'safety' procedures
5. Intolerance of discomfort	Committing to goals, challenging 'catastrophic' cognitions
6. Dependence	Daring to gradually act independently
7. Relapse prevention	Personally constructed self-help 'manual', utilising key points from therapy and drawing on self-help books and computer assisted material

Post-traumatic stress disorder

A.

(1)   Have you ever been involved in a very serious accident, incident or assault that still plays on your mind?

If more than one trauma is reported: Which one of these affected you most?

(2)   How did you react when it happened?

If unclear: Were you afraid or did you feel terrified or helpless?

In order to meet criterion A the person must have both objectively experienced an extreme event A(1) and felt intense fear, helplessness or horror at the time A(2).

B.

i   Do you have distressing memories or pictures of the incident popping into your mind?
ii   Do you have distressing nightmares of the incident?
iii   Do you ever feel that you are not just remembering the incident but that you feel like it is happening again and lose some awareness of where you are, what you are doing?
iv   Do you come across any reminders of the incident that cause you to get very upset?
v   Do you get any physical symptoms such as breathing heavily, heart racing, sweating when you come across reminders?

In order to meet criterion B at least one of the symptoms in this category must be endorsed.

C.

i   Do you try to block thoughts/images and avoid conversations about the incident?
ii   Do you avoid activities, places or people that bring back memories of the incident?
iii   Is there any big gap in your memory of the incident that you don't remember even though it was at a time that you were conscious?
iv   Have you lost interest in or stopped bothering with things you used to do that you enjoyed?
v   Have you felt that you are not connecting with others, more than just a bit out of synch?

vi   Do you feel flat, unable to feel warm to people?
vii Do you have a sense that you are going to die young, by a particular age?

In order to meet criterion C at least three of the symptoms in this category must be endorsed.

D.

i   Are you having difficulty falling or staying asleep?
ii   Have you been having outbursts of anger or snapping?
iii Do you have trouble concentrating sufficiently to read or watch TV?
iv   Are you on guard a lot of the time, keep checking on things?
v   Are you easily startled, taking more than seconds to calm down?

In order to meet criterion D at least two of the symptoms in this category must be endorsed and these symptoms must represent a change in functioning from before the trauma.

For a diagnosis of PTSD not only must the client have at least one intrusion, three avoidance and two disordered arousal symptoms but the symptoms must have lasted at least a month and significantly interfered with their working or domestic life.

Conceptualisation – suggest developed a 'dodgy alarm' (amygdala) that goes off (a) at any reminder, (b) anything not exactly the way you want it to be and (c) unexpected noises or sudden movements. Client reacts as if in a 'war zone', making communication with others very strained.

Post-traumatic stress disorder Sat Nav

Therapeutic targets	Treatment strategies
1. Taking seriously the sense of vulnerability/threat	Distinguishing 'real' from 'false' alarms, elaboration of similarities/differences in response to reminders
2. Self-blame	Accepting that responses are a normal response to an abnormal situation
3. Nightmares	Updating account of trauma and correcting the fantasy of an even worse outcome
4. Flashbacks	Detached mindfulness, writing an updated account of the trauma or constructing and listening to updated account on audiotape
5. Avoidance	Daring to gradually venture into the land of approach
6. Isolation	Building bridges with others, communication guidelines, anger control
7. Mood	Use of MOOD chart to manage mood
8. Relapse prevention	Personally constructed self-help 'manual', utilising key points from therapy and drawing on self-help books and computer assisted material

Social phobia

1   When you are or might be in the spotlight, say in a group of people or eating/writing in front of others, do you immediately get anxious or nervous?

2   Do you think you are much more anxious than other people when the focus is on you?

3   Do you think that you are more afraid of social situations than you should be?

4   Do you avoid social situations out of a fear of embarrassing or humiliating yourself?

5   Do these social anxieties bother you?

If the client answered yes to each of the above five questions it is likely that they are suffering from social phobia.

Conceptualisation – present a formulation that makes sense to the client and is consistent with the CBT model. Examples:

(a) 'It is as if people with social phobia think that they are at the centre of a circle, others are on the edge of the circle looking at them marking them out of 10. If it was really like that no one would do anything, I'd be like a frightened rabbit frozen in car headlights on a country road.'

(b) 'Can you be sure that the story you carry around of how others think about you is correct? Maybe different people have different stories?'

(c) 'Who says you have to be perfect socially, to be acceptable; politicians are never short of words but who trusts them?' When you think of people you like are they really the most socially skilled people?'

Social phobia Sat Nav

Therapeutic targets	Treatment strategies
1. Perception of what others think about them	Revisiting onset of belief that others negatively evaluate them and consequences, contrasted with utility of previous beliefs/assumptions
2. Information processing biases	Vigilance for all or nothing thinking, mindreading and inappropriate moral imperatives. Use of MOOD chart
3. Theory of mind (ToM)	Poor fit between client's official version of what is necessary to be acceptable to others with the actual behaviour of those they like. Rescripting ToM
4. 'Adolescent' self	Comforting, re-educating the 'adolescent' self that emerges in social situations. Coping self-statements – preparing for the stressor, encountering the stressor, coping with feeling overwhelmed, post-mortem
5. Social skills	Teaching client (a) how to keep a conversation going and to talk themselves using the headings 'general', 'specific', 'feeling' and (b) the greater importance of non-verbal skills
6. Avoidance	Graded exposure to avoided situations
7. Relapse prevention	Personally constructed self-help 'manual', utilising key points from therapy and drawing on self-help books and computer assisted material

Appendix E
MOOD thought record

_Mo_nitor mood	_O_bserve thinking	_O_bjective thinking	_D_ecide what to do and do it

Appendix F
Panic diary

1. Date   Time began   Time to reach worst

Physical symptoms ....

What I thought? ....

What I did? ....

How bad on a scale (0–10) where 10 would be the worst attack I have ever had?

....

2. Date   Time began   Time to reach worst

Physical symptoms ....

What I thought? ....

What I did? ....

How bad on a scale (0–10) where 10 would be the worst attack I have ever had?

....

3. Date   Time began   Time to reach worst

Physical symptoms ....

What I thought? ....

What I did? ....

How bad on a scale (0–10) where 10 would be the worst attack I have ever had?

....

Appendix G

Therapist Competence Screen

1 Did the therapist collaborate with the client in addressing his/her pressing concerns?
   Yes   No
2 Did the therapist focus on a therapeutic target appropriate for the disorder (first column in Sat Nav)?
   Yes   No
3 Did the therapist employ an appropriate treatment strategy for the targeted problem (second column in Sat Nav)?
   Yes   No
4 Did the therapist negotiate a homework assignment that addressed the therapeutic target and integrated new learning from the session?
   Yes   No   Unsure
5 Was there a review of homework?
   Yes   No

A positive response to each of the five questions indicates a probable at least minimal level of therapist competence.

Appendix H
The First Step Questionnaire

This questionnaire is a first step in identifying what you might be suffering from and pointing you in the right direction. In answering each question just make your best guess, don't think about your response too much, there are no right or wrong answers.

1.	Yes	No	Don't know
During the past month have you often been bothered by feeling depressed or hopeless?			
During the past month have you often been bothered by little interest or pleasure in doing things?			
Is this something with which you would like help?			

2.	Yes	No	Don't know
Do you have unexpected panic attacks, a sudden rush of intense fear or anxiety?			
Do you avoid situations in which the panic attacks might occur?			
Is this something with which you would like help?			

3.	Yes	No	Don't know
In your life, have you ever had any experience that was so frightening, horrible or upsetting that, in the past month, you			
i. Have had nightmares about it or thought about it when you did not want to?			

ii. Tried hard not to think about it or went out of your way to avoid situations that reminded you of it?			
iii. Were constantly on guard, watchful, or easily startled?			
iv. Felt numb or detached from others, activities, or your surroundings?			
Is this something with which you would like help?			

4.	Yes	No	Don't know
Are you a worrier?			
Do you worry about everything?			
Has the worrying been excessive (more days than not) or uncontrollable in the last 6 months?			
Is this something with which you would like help?			

5.	Yes	No	Don't know
When you are or might be in the spotlight say in a group of people or eating/writing in front of others do you immediately get anxious or nervous?			
Do you avoid social situations out of a fear of embarrassing or humiliating yourself?			
Is this something with which you would like help?			

6.	Yes	No	Don't know
Are you bothered by thoughts, images or impulses that keep going over in your mind?			
Do you try to block these thoughts, images or impulses by thinking or doing something?			
Is this something with which you would like help?			

7.	Yes	No	Don't know
Do you go on binges where you eat very large amounts of food in a short period?			
Do you do anything special, such as vomiting, go on a strict diet to prevent gaining weight from the binge?			
Is this something with which you would like help?			

8.	Yes	No	Don't know
Have you felt you should cut down on your alcohol/drug?			
Have people got annoyed with you about your drinking/drug taking?			
Have you felt guilty about your drinking/drug use?			
Do you drink/use drugs before midday?			
Is this something with which you would like help?			

9.	Yes	No	Don't know
Do you ever hear things other people don't hear, or see things they don't see?			
Do you ever feel like someone is spying on you or plotting to hurt you?			
Do you have any ideas that you don't like to talk about because you are afraid other people will think you are crazy?			
Is this something with which you would like help?			

10.	Yes	No	Don't know
Have there been times, lasting at least a few days when you were unusually high, talking a lot, sleeping little?			
Did others notice that there was something different about you? If you answered 'yes', what did they say?			
Is this something with which you would like help?			

Appendix I
Recovered but . . .

1   I need to be alert for possible triggers to relapse, which are likely to involve:
2   I need to identify what I have started thinking again, which will likely involve:
3   I need to identify what I have started doing again, which will likely involve:
4   I need to remind myself to apply what worked last time, but at the earliest opportunity so that a slip does not become a full-blown relapse. What worked best last time was:
5   I need to expect slips and learn from them, so that the gap between slips gets gradually longer.
6   I have to be alert for black and white thinking, e.g. 'I am either cured or suffering from full . . .'
7   I need to remind myself that it is only a question of regaining lost ground; I am not back at square one.
8   In the event of a slip I must utilise not only the survival manual, but other resources such as self-help books, computer assisted therapy, a therapist, GP, a good friend/family member.

References

Abramowitz, J.S., Storch, E.A., Keeley, M. and Cordell, E. (2007) Obsessive-compulsive disorder with comorbid major depression: what is the role of cognitive factors? *Behaviour Research and Therapy*, 45, 2257–2267.

Agosti, V. and Ocepek-Welikon, K. (1997) The efficacy of imipramine and psychotherapy in early onset chronic depression. A reanalysis of the National Institute for Mental Health Treatment of Depression Collaborative Research Program. *Journal of Affective Disorders*, 43, 181–186.

Alford, B.A. and Beck A.T. (1997) *The Integrative Power of Cognitive Therapy.* New York: Guilford Press.

American Psychiatric Association (1995) *Diagnostic and Statistical Manual of Mental Disorders*, 4th edn, *Primary Care.* Washington, DC: APA.

American Psychiatric Association (2000) *Diagnostic and Statistical Manual of Mental Disorders*, 4th edn, Text Revision (DSM-IV-TR). Washington, DC: APA.

Anderson, R.A. and Rees, C.S. (2007) Group versus individual cognitive-behavioural treatment for obsessive-compulsive disorder: a controlled trial. *Behaviour Research and Therapy*, 45, 123–127.

Arroll, B., Goodyear-Smith, F., Kerse, N., Fishman, T. and Gunn, J. (2005) Effect of the addition of a 'help' question to two screening questions on specificity for diagnosis of depression in general practice: diagnostic validity study. *British Medical Journal*, 331, 884–886.

Barlow, D.H. and Cerny, J.A. (1988) *Psychological Treatment of Panic.* New York: Guilford Press.

Barlow, D.H. and Craske, M.G. (1994) *Mastery of Your Anxiety and Panic*, Vol II. Albany, NY: Graywind.

Barlow, D.H. and Craske, M.G. (2007) *Mastery of Your Anxiety and Panic*, 4th edn. Oxford: Oxford University Press.

Beach, S.R.H. and O'Leary, K.D. (1986) The treatment of depression in the context of marital discord. *Behaviour Therapy*, 17, 43–49.

Beck, A.T. (1967 Depression: clinical, theoretical and experimental aspects. New York: Hoeber.

Beck, A.T. (1987) Cognitive models of depression. *Journal of Cognitive Psychotherapy, An International Quarterly*, 1, 5–37.

Beck, A.T. (2006) How an anomalous finding led to a new system of psychotherapy. *Nature Medicine*, 12, 1139–1141.

Beck, A.T. and Steer, R. (1993) *Manual for the Beck Anxiety Inventory*. San Antonio, TX: Psychological Corporation.

Beck, A.T., Ward, C.H., Mendelson, M., Mock, J.E. and Erbaugh, J.K. (1962) Reliability of psychiatrics diagnoses: a study of consistency of clinical judgements and ratings. *American Journal of Psychiatry*, 119, 351–357.

Beck, A.T., Rush, A.J, Shaw, B.F. and Emery, G. (1979) *Cognitive Therapy of Depression*. New York: Guilford Press.

Beck, A.T., Emery, G. and Greenberg, R.L. (1985) *Anxiety Disorders and Phobias: A Cognitive Perspective*. New York: Basic Books.

Beck, A.T., Steer, R.A. and Brown, G.K. (1996) *Manual for Beck Depression Inventory-II*. San Antonio, TX: Psychological Corporation.

Blanchard, E.B. and Hickling, E.J. (1997) *After the Crash: Assessment and Treatment of Motor Vehicle Accident Survivors*. Washington, DC: American Psychological Association.

Bradley, R., Greene, J., Russ, E., Dutra, L. and Westen, D. (2005) A multidimensional meta-analysis of psychotherapy for PTSD. *American Journal of Psychiatry*, 162, 214–227.

Brewin, C.R., Dalgleish, T. and Joseph, S. (1996) A dual representation theory of posttraumatic stress disorder. *Psychological Review*, 103, 670–686.

Brewin, C.R., Andrews, B. and Valentine, J.D. (2000) Meta-analysis of risk factors for post-traumatic stress disorder in trauma exposed adults. *Journal of Consulting and Clinical Psychology*, 68: 748–766.

Brown, G.K., Have, T.T., Henriques, G.R., Xie, S.X., Hollander, J.E. and Beck, A.T. (2005) Cognitive therapy for the prevention of suicide attempts: a randomized control trial. *Journal of the American Medical Association*, 294, 563–570.

Brown, T.A., DiNardo, P. and Barlow, D.H. (2004) *Anxiety Disorders Interview Schedule (ADIS IV)*. USA: Oxford University Press.

Burns, D. (1999) *Feeling Good: The New Mood Therapy*. New York: Avon Books.

Butler, A.C., Brown, G.K., Beck, A.T. and Grisham, J.R. (2002) Assessment of dysfunctional beliefs in borderline personality disorder. *Behaviour Research and Therapy*, 40, 1231–1240.

Butler, A.C., Chapman, J.E., Forman, E.M. and Beck A.T. (2006) The empirical status of cognitive-behavioral therapy: a review of meta-analyses. *Clinical Psychology Review*, 26, 17–31.

Chambless, D.L. and Ollendick, T.H. (2001) Empirically supported psychological interventions: controversies and evidence. *Annual Review of Psychology*, 52, 685–716.

Chambless, D.L., Caputo, G.S., Bright, P. and Gallagher, R. (1984) Assessment of fear in agoraphobics, the Bodily Sensation Questionnaire and the Agoraphobic Cognitions Questionnaire. *Journal of Consulting and Clinical Psychology*, 52, 1090–1097.

Champion, L.A. and Power, M.J. (1995) Social and cognitive approaches to depression. Towards a new synthesis. *British Journal of Clinical Psychology*, 34, 485–503.

Clark, D.M. (1986) A cognitive model of panic. *Behaviour Research and Therapy*, 24, 461–470.

Clark, D.M., Salkovskis, P.M., Hackmann, A., Wells, A., Ludgate, J. and Gelder, M. (1999) Brief cognitive therapy for panic disorder: a randomised controlled trial. *Journal of Consulting and Clinical Psychology*, 67, 583–589.

Clark, D.M., Ehlers, A., McManus, F. *et al.* (2003) Cognitive therapy versus fluoxetine in generalised social phobia: a randomised placebo-controlled trial. *Journal of Consulting and Clinical Psychology* 71(6), 1058–1067.

Colman, I., Ploubidis, G.B., Wadsworth, M.E.J., Jones, P.B. and Croudace, T.J. (2007) A longitudinal typology of symptoms of depression and anxiety over the life course. *Biological Psychiatry*, 62, 1265–1271.

Connor, K.M., Davidson, J.R.T., Churchill, L.E., Sherwood, A., Weisler, R.H. and Foa, E. (2000) Psychometric properties of the Social Phobia Inventory (SPIN). *British Journal of Psychiatry*, 176, 379–386.

Craske, M.G., Barlow, D.H. and Meadows, E.A. (2000) *Mastery of your Anxiety and Panic: Therapist Guide for Anxiety, Panics and Agoraphobia (MAP-3).* San Antonio, TX: Graywind/Psychological Corporation.

Department of Health (2001) *Treatment Choice in Psychological Therapies and Counselling: Evidence Based Clinical Practice Guideline.* London.

Department of Health (2007) *Cognitive and behavioural therapy (CBT) for people with depression and anxiety. What skills can service users expect their therapists to have?* (Authors Roth, A.D. and Pilling, S.). London.

Dugas, M.J., Ladouceur, R., Leger, E., Freeston, M.H., Langlois, F. and Provencher, M.D. (2003) Group cognitive-behavioural therapy for generalised anxiety disorder: treatment outcome and long-term follow up. *Journal of Consulting and Clinical Psychology*, 71, 821–825.

Dugas, M.J., Savard, P., Gaudet, A., Turcotte, J., Laugesen, N., Robichaud., M., Francis, K. and Koerner, N. (2007) Can the components of a cognitive model predict the severity of generalised anxiety disorder. *Behaviour Therapy and Research*, 38, 169–178.

Elkin, I., Shea, T., Watkins, J.T., Imber, S.D. and Sotsky, S.M. (1989) National Institute of Mental Health Treatment of Depression Collaborative Research Program: general effectiveness of treatments. *Archives of General Psychiatry*, 46, 971–982.

Engelhard, I., Arntz, A. and van den Hout, M.A. (2007) Low specificity of symptoms on the post-traumatic stress disorder (PTSD) symptom scale: a comparison of individuals with PTSD, individuals with other anxiety disorders and individuals without psychopathology. *British Journal of Cinical Psychology*, 46, 449–456.

Etkin, A. and Wager, T.D. (2007) Functional neuroimaging of anxiety: a meta-analysis of emotional processing in PTSD, social anxiety disorder and specific phobia. *American Journal of Psychiatry*, 164, 1476–1488.

Ewing, J.A. (1984) Detecting alcoholism: the CAGE Questionnaire. *JAMA*, 252, 1905–1907.

Fales, C.F., Barch, D.M., Rundle, M.M., Mintun, M.A., Snyder, A.Z., Chen, J.D., Mathews, J. and Sheline, Y.I. (2008) Altered emotional interference processing in affective and cognitive-control brain circuitry in major depression. *Biological Psychiatry*, 63, 377–384.

Fineberg, N.A., Saxena, S., Zohar, J. and Craig, K.J. (2007) Obsessive-compulsive disorders: boundary issues. *CNS Spectrums*, 12, 359–375.

First, M.B., Spitzer, R.L., Gibbon, M. and Williams, J.B.W. (1997) *Structured Clinical Interview for DSM-IV Axis 1 Disorders – Clinician Version (SCID-CV).* Washington, DC: American Psychiatric Press.

Foa, E.B. and Rothbaum, B.O. (1998) *Treating the Trauma of Rape*. New York: Guilford Press.

Foa, E.B., Cashman, L., Jaycox, L. and Perry, J. (1997) The validation of a self-report measure of posttraumatic stress disorder: the posttraumatic diagnostic scale. *Psychological Assessment*, 9, 445–451.

Foa, E.B., Ehlers, A., Clark, D.M., Tolin, D.F. and Orsillo, S.M. (1999) The Post-traumatic Cognitions Inventory (PTCI): Development and validation. *Psychological Assessment*, 11, 303–314.

Freeston, M.H., Ladoucer, R., Gagnon, F., Thibodeau, M., Rheaume, J., Letarte, H. and Bujold, A. (1997) Cognitive-behavioural treatment of obsessive thoughts: a controlled study. *Journal of Consulting and Clinical Psychology*, 65, 405–413.

Goodman, W., Price, L., Rasmussen, S. and Mazure, C. (1989) The Yale-Brown Obsessive Compulsive Scale. Development, use and reliability. *Archives of General Psychiatry*, 46, 1006–1011.

Hamilton, K.E. and Dobson, K.S. (2002) Cognitive therapy of depression: pretreatment patient predictors of outcome. *Clinical Psychology Review*, 22, 875–893.

Hirshfeld-Becker, D.R., Micco, J.A., Simoes, N.A. and Henin, A. (2008) High risk studies and developmental antecedents of anxiety disorders. *American Journal of Medical Genetics*, (Epub ahead of print).

Hooley, J.M., Orley, J. and Teasdale, J.D. (1986) Levels of expressed emotion and relapse in depressed patients. *British Journal of Psychiatry*, 148, 642–647.

Jacobson, N.S. and Truax, P. (1991) Clinical significance: a statistical approach to defining meaningful change in psychotherapy research. *Journal of Consulting and Clinical Psychology*, 59, 12–19.

Kampman, M., Keijsers, G.P.J., Hoogduin, C.A.L. and Hendriks, G. (2008) Outcome prediction of cognitive behaviour therapy for panic disorder: initial symptom severity is predictive for treatment outcome, comorbid anxiety or depressive disorder, cluster C personality disorders and initial motivation are not. *Behavioural and Cognitive Psychotherapy*, 36, 99–112.

Kessler, R.C., Sonnega, A., Bromet, E., Hughes, M. and Nelson, C.B. (1995) Post-traumatic stress disorder in the National Comorbidity Survey. *Archives of General Psychiatry*, 52, 1048–1060.

Kessler, R.C., Berglund, P., Demler, O., Jin, R., Merikangas, K.R., Rush, A.J., Walters, E.E. and Wang, P.S. (2003) The epidemiology of major depressive disorder: results from the National Comorbidity Survey Replication (NCS-R). *Journal of the American Medical Association*, 289, 3095–3105.

Kroenke, K., Spitzer, R.L. and Williams, J.B. (2001) The PHQ-9: validity of a brief depression measure. *Journal of General Internal Medicine*, 16, 606–613.

Kroenke, K., Spitzer, R.L. and Williams, J.B. (2007) Anxiety disorders in primary care: prevalence, impairment, comorbidity and detection. *Annals of Internal Medicine*, 146, 317–325.

Kuyken, W., Kurzer, N., DeRubeis, R.J., Beck, A.T. and Brown, G.K. (2001) Response to cognitive therapy in depression the role of maladaptive beliefs and personality disorders. *Journal of Consulting and Clinical Psychology*, 69, 560–566.

Kuyken, W., Fothergill, C.D., Musa, M. and Chadwick, P. (2005) The reliability and quality of cognitive case formulation. *Behaviour Research and Therapy*, 43, 1187–1201.

Ladouceur, R., Blais, F., Freeston, M.H., Leger, E., Gagnon, F. and Tibodeau, N.

(2000) Efficacy of cognitive-behavioural treatment for generalised anxiety disorder: evaluation in a controlled clinical trial. *Journal of Consulting and Clinical Psychology*, 68, 957–964.

LeDoux, J.E. (1998) *The Emotional Brain: The Mysterious Underpinnings of Emotional Life*. London: Weidenfeld and Nicolson.

Linehan, M.M. (1993) *Skills Training Manual for Treating Borderline Personality Disorder*. New York: Guilford Press.

McMillan, D., Gilbody, S., Beresford, E. and Neilly, L. (2007) Can we predict suicide and non-fatal self-harm with the Beck Hopelessness Scale? A meta-analysis. *Psychological Medicine*, 37, 769–778.

Maercker, A., Zollner, T., Menning, H., Rabe, S. and Karl, A. (2006) Dresden PTSD treatment study: randomised control trial of motor vehicle accident survivors. *BMC Psychiatry*, 6, 6–29.

Meichenbaum, D. (1985) *Stress Inoculation Training*. London: Pergamon Press.

Miller, B.P. and Giordano, R. (2007) Creating a suicide risk assessment tool for use in the Emergency Department. American Psychiatric Association Annual Meeting, 21 May.

Monk, C.S., Telzer, E.H. and Mogg, K. (2008) Amygdala and ventrolateral prefrontal cortex activation to masked angry faces in children and adolescents with generalised anxiety disorder. *Archives of General Psychiatry*, 65, 568–576.

Murphy, G.E. (1985) A conceptual framework for the choice of interventions in cognitive therapy. *Cognitive Therapy and Research*, 15, 127–134.

Neuner, F., Schaver, M., Klaschik, C., Karunakera, U. and Elbert, T. (2004) A comparison of narrative exposure therapy, support counselling and psycho education for treating post-traumatic stress disorder in an African refugee settlement. *Journal of Consulting and Clinical Psychology*, 72, 579–587.

Nezu, A.M. (1986) Efficacy of a social problem-solving therapy approach for unipolar depression. *Journal of Consulting and Clinical Psychology*, 54, 196–202.

Nezu, A.M. and Perri, M.G. (1989) Problem-solving therapy for unipolar depression: an initial dismantling investigation. *Journal of Consulting and Clinical Psychology*, 57, 408–413.

Nezu, A.M., Nezu, C.M. and Perri, M.G. (1989) *Problem-Solving Therapy for Depression: Theory Research and Clinical Guidelines*. New York: John Wiley and Sons.

NICE (National Institute for Health and Clinical Excellence) (2004) Depression: The management of depression in primary and secondary care. Available online at www.nice.org.uk.

Obsessive Compulsive Cognitions Working Group (2005) Psychometric validation of the Obsessive Belief Questionnaire. *Behaviour Research and Therapy*, 43, 1527–1542.

Prins, A., Ouimette, P. and Kimerling, R. (2004) The primary care PTSD screen (PC-PTSD): development and operating characteristics *Primary Care Psychiatry*, 9, 9–14.

Rapee, R.M. and Heimberg, R.G. (1997) A cognitive-behavioral model of social anxiety in social phobia. *Behaviour Research and Therapy*, 35, 741–756.

Resick, P.A. and Schnicke, M.K. (1993) *Cognitive Processing Therapy for Rape Victims*. Newbury Park, CA: Sage.

Rogers, R. (2001) *Handbook of Diagnostic and Structured Interviewing*. New York: Guilford Press.

Rosqvist, J. (2005) *Exposure Treatments for Anxiety Disorders*. New York: Routledge.

Ross, M. and Scott, M. (1985) An evaluation of individual and group cognitive therapy in the treatment of depression in an inner city health centre. *Journal of the Royal College of General Practitioners*, 35, 239–242.

Roth, A. and Fonagy, P. (2005) *What Works For Whom?* New York: Guilford Press.

Rush, A.J., Beck, A.T., Kovacs, M. and Hollon, S. (1977) Comparative efficacy of cognitive therapy and pharmacotherapy in the treatment of depressed outpatients. *Cognitive Therapy and Research*, 1, 17–38.

Salkovskis, P. (2008) Twenty obsessional years, compulsive research with a few doubts feels just right. BABCP Annual Conference, University of Edinburgh, 18 July.

Salkovskis, P.M., Clark, D.M. and Gelder, M.G. (1996) Cognition-behaviour links in the persistence of panic. *Behaviour Research and Therapy*, 34, 453–458.

Saxena, S. (2003) Neuroimaging and the pathophysiology of obsessive compulsive disorder. In Fu, C.H., Senior, C., Russell, T.A., Weinberger, D. and Murray, R. (eds) *Neuroimaging in Psychiatry*. London: Martin Dunitz.

Scott, M.J. (2008) *Moving On After Trauma: A Guide for Survivors, Family and Friends*. London: Routledge.

Scott, M.J. and Stradling, S.G. (1990) Group cognitive therapy for depression produces clinically significant reliable change in community-based settings. *Behavioural Psychotherapy*, 18, 1–19.

Scott, M.J. and Stradling, S.G. (1994) Post-traumatic stress disorder without the trauma. *British Journal of Clinical Psychology*, 33, 71–74.

Scott, M.J. and Stradling, S.G. (2006) *Counselling for Post-traumatic Stress Disorder*, 3rd edn. London: Sage Publications.

Shaw, B.F., Elkin, I., Yamagughi, J., Olmsted, M., Vallis, T.M., Dobson, K.S., Lowery, A., Sotsky, S.M., Watkins, J.T. and Imber, S.D. (1999) Therapist competence ratings in relation to clinical outcome in cognitive therapy of depression. *Journal of Consulting and Clinical Psychology*, 67, 837–846.

Silverman, W.H. (1996) Cookbooks, manuals and paint-by-numbers: psychotherapy in the 90's. *Psychotherapy*, 33, 36–40.

Simons, G.E. and Savarino, J. (2007) Suicide attempts among patients starting depression treatment with medications or psychotherapy. *American Journal of Psychiatry*, 164, 1029–1034.

Smith, E.W.L. (1995) A passionate, rational response to the 'manualization' of psychotherapy. *Psychotherapy Bulletin*, 30, 36–40.

Solomon, D.A., Keller, M.B., Leon, A.C., Mueller, T.I., Lavori, P.W., Shea, M.T., Coryell, W., Warshaw, M., Turvey, C., Maser, J.D. and Endicott, Y. (2001) Multiple recurrences of major depressive disorder. *American Journal of Psychiatry*, 157, 229–233.

Spitzer, R.L., Kroenke, K., Williams, J.B.W. and Lowe, B. (2006) A brief measure for assessing generalised anxiety disorder the GAD-7. *Archives of Internal Medicine*, 166, 1092–1097.

Stein, M.B. and Stein, D.J. (2008) Social anxiety disorder. *Lancet*, 371, 1115–1125.

Stobie, B., Taylor, T. and Quigley, A. (2007) 'Contents may vary': a pilot study of treatment histories of OCD patients. *Behavioural and Cognitive Psychotherapy*, 35, 273–282.

Torres, A.R., Prince, M.J., Bebbington, P.E., Bhugra, D., Brugha, T.S., Farrell, M., Jenkins, R., Lewis, G., Meltzer, H. and Singleton, N. (2006) Obsessive-compulsive disorder: prevalence, comorbidity, impact and help-seeking in the British National Psychiatric Morbidity Survey 2000. *American Journal of Psychiatry*, 163, 1978–1985.

Tungstrom, S., Soderberg, P. and Armelius, B. (2005) Special section on the GAF: relationship between the Global Assessment of Functioning and other DSM axes in routine clinical work. *Psychiatric Services*, 56, 439–443.

Wade, W.A., Treat, T.A. and Stuart, G.L. (1998) Transporting an empirically supported treatment for panic disorder to a service clinic setting: a benchmarking strategy. *Journal of Consulting and Clinical Psychology*, 66, 231–239.

Weathers, F.W., Litz, B.T., Herman, D.S., Huska, J.A. and Keane, T.M. (1993) The PTSD Checklist (PCL): reliability, validity and diagnostic utility. Paper presented at the Annual Meeting of International Society for Traumatic Stress Studies, San Antonio, TX, October 1993.

Weerasekera, P. (1996) Multiperspective case formulation: a step towards treatment integration. Malabar, FL: Krieger Publishing.

Weertman, A., Arntx, A., Schouten, E. and Dreesen, L. (2005) Influences of beliefs and personality disorders on treatment outcome in anxiety patients. *Journal of Consulting and Clinical Psychology*, 73, 936–944.

Wegner, D.M., Schneider, D.J., Carter, S.R. and White, T.L. (1987) Paradoxical effects of thought suppression. *Journal of Personality and Social Psychology*, 53, 5–13.

Weissman, A. and Beck, A.T. (1978) Development and validation of the Dysfunctional Attitude Scale paper presented at the Annual Convention of the Association for the Advancement of Behavior Therapy, Chicago.

Wells, A. (1994) A multidimensional measure of worry: development and preliminary validation of the Anxious Thoughts Inventory. *Anxiety, Stress and Coping*, 6, 289–299.

Wells, A. (1997) *Cognitive Therapy of Anxiety Disorders: A Practice Manual and Conceptual Guide*. Chichester: John Wiley and Sons.

Wells, A. and Sembi, S. (2004) Metacognitive therapy for PTSD: a core treatment manual. *Cognitive and Behavioral Practice*, 11, 365–377.

Wells, A., Stopa, L. and Clark, D.M. (1993) The Social Cognitions Questionnaire. Unpublished. (The psychometric properties of the SCQ are in Wells (1997), p. 29.)

White, J., Keenan, M. and Brooks, N. (1992) Stress control: a controlled comparative investigation of large group therapy for generalised anxiety disorder. *Behavioural Psychotherapy*, 20, 97–114.

Whittal, M.L., Rachman, S. and McLean, P.D. (2002) Psychosocial treatment for OCD. In Simos, G. (ed.) *Cognitive Behaviour Therapy: A Guide for the Practising Clinician*. London: Brunnner Routledge.

Young, J.E. (1994) *Cognitive Therapy for Personality Disorders: A Schema-Focused Approach*. Revised Edition. Sarasota: Professional Resource Press.

Young, J. and Beck, A.T. (1980) Cognitive Therapy Rating Scale: rating manual. Unpublished manuscript. Philadelphia: Centre for Cognitive Therapy, University of Pennsylvania.

Young, J.E., Beck, A.T. and Weinberger, A. (2001) 'Depression'. In *Clinical Handbook of Psychological Disorders*, 3rd edn. New York: Guiford Press.

Zimmerman, M. and Mattia, J.I. (1999) Is posttraumatic stress disorder underdiagnosed in routine clinical settings? *Journal of Nervous and Mental Disease*, 187, 420–428.

Zimmerman, M. and Mattia, J.I. (2000) Principal and additional DSM-IV disorders for which outpatients seek treatment. *Psychiatric Services*, 51, 1299–1304.

Zimmerman, M. and Mattia, J.I. (2001) The Psychiatric Diagnostic Screening Questionnaire: development, reliability and validity. *Comprehensive Psychiatry*, 42, 175–189.

Zimmerman, M., McGlinchey, J.B., Chelminski, I. and Young, D. (2008) Diagnostic co-morbidity in 2300 psychiatric out-patients presenting for treatment evaluated with a semi-structured diagnostic interview. *Psychological Medicine*, 38, 199–210.

Index